· WOOD PROJECTS FOR THE HOME ·

Created and
designed by
the editorial staff
of ORTHO Books

Text and drawings by
Ron Hildebrand

Graphic design by
James Stockton

Consultation on project
design & construction by
Diane Crocker

Photography by
David Fischer

Photographic styling by
Sara Slavin

Final illustrations by
Cyndie Clark-Huegel

Ortho Books

Publisher
Robert L. Iacopi

Editorial Director
Min S. Yee

Managing Editor
Anne Coolman

Horticultural Editor
Michael D. Smith

Production Editor
Barbara J. Ferguson

Editorial Assistant
Maureen V. Meehan

Administrative Assistant
Judith C. Pillon

Copyediting by
Joan Lichterman
Editcetera
Berkeley, CA

Typography by
Terry Robinson & Co.
San Francisco, CA

Color Separations by
Color Tech Corp.
Redwood City, CA

Address all inquiries to:
Ortho Books
Chevron Chemical Company
Consumer Products Division
575 Market Street
San Francisco, CA 94105

1 2 3 4 5 6 7 8 9 10

Printed in August, 1980

ISBN 0-917102-85-1

Library of Congress Catalog
Card Number 80-66343

Acknowledgements

Projects designed by
Ron Hildebrand
Mike Landis
Diane Crocker

Projects built by
Ron Hildebrand
Mike Landis
Steve Crocker
Jeff Borcich

Assistant builders
Mark Walheim
Mark Dawson

Redwood supplied by
California Redwood Association
San Francisco, CA

Hardwood supplied by
MacBeath Lumber Company
Distribution Yards located at:

2150 Oakdale Ave.
San Francisco, CA 94124

930 Ashby Avenue
Berkeley, CA 94710

7653 Telegraph Road
Montebello, CA 90640

1576 South 300 West
Salt Lake City, UT 84115

• WOOD PROJECTS FOR THE HOME •

• WORKING WITH WOOD •

Working with wood is a time-honored American tradition. While modern tools have made woodworking faster, easier, and more precise, the satisfaction is the same whether you use hand tools or power tools. These projects will provide a basis for you to enjoy this tradition to its fullest.

You can build any project in this book. If you're a complete novice to woodworking, you'll find projects tailor-made to introduce you to the process and its pleasures. If you've tried your hand at woodworking before, you'll find exciting challenges here. And if you're a skilled woodworker, there are plenty of projects to pique your appetite.

Any wood project, from the simplest set of children's blocks to the most complex cabinet, starts with the first saw cut. With each new cut you gain experience, and that's what woodworking is all about. We've planned this book with the hope that you will take your resources at hand and develop your skills and your craftsmanship.

The designs of these projects can be followed exactly, or changed to suit your needs and your skills. The important thing is to use these designs and specifications as a basis for whatever you build, and go on from there.

HOW TO USE THIS BOOK

The projects in this book are categorized by use, not by level of skill. While we haven't covered all aspects of woodworking, the techniques chapter explains all the processes used in building these projects. Throughout the construction steps you will be referred to specific parts of that section.

In many cases we describe alternative methods and tools that can be used for various procedures. For example, notches can be made in several ways and don't require a router; drawers can be assembled in more than one way, and different methods are noted; a portable circular saw can be used for cuts we made on a radial arm or table saw; butt joints can be used instead of miter joints. If you want to try out a new tool or technique, try your hand first on a simple project. Then move on to something larger or more complex. The most important thing is to follow your own interests, level of patience, and skill, and to use the tools you are most comfortable with.

A Word About Tools

The tools you use are less important than the skill with which you wield them, for the performance of a tool is governed primarily by the skill of the person using it, not by its raw capabilities.

Fine furniture was built for centuries prior to the development of power tools, and a whole kind of craftsmanship developed surrounding these tools. The Industrial Revolution made woodworking faster, easier and more precise, bringing with it another type of woodworking skill. Depending on what type of skills you choose to develop and what kind of tools you want to use, you can pursue your projects either way. Some of our projects were designed for using hand tools—such as the traditional American sawbuck table—and all can be built

Before the advent of electric power tools all woodworking operations were done with hand tools. Using hand tools usually takes a little longer and you have to be careful, but the results can be equally satisfactory. In the photos, we show the author performing the same operation using a hand tool and a power tool, rounding over the edge of a piece of cherry with a rasp (left) and with an electric router (right).

with them. In some cases, it will be more time-consuming and even more difficult, but certainly worth the effort if this is your interest.

If you prefer to use power tools but don't have and can't afford them, there are various options to pursue: borrow friends' tools; see whether there are cooperative workshops in your area; an adult high school, community college, park district, or community center that has a wood shop; or a tool-lending library. Or consider the possibilities of developing hand-tool craftsmanship.

Whatever your tools, make sure they are in good working condition. Dull tools make the work not only tedious and time-consuming, but dangerous as well. You'll save a lot of time and frustration if you have what you need before you begin, and if your tools are accessible yet out of your way once you've begun.

Safety should never be taken for granted. Goggles or safety glasses will keep nail chips, splinters, sawdust, and finishes out of your eyes, and should always be worn when working with wood. A mask will keep sawdust out of your mouth, nose, and lungs. Gloves should be used when handling heavy boards but not when operating power equipment, because they can get caught. Similarly, loose clothing should never be worn around power equipment.

Starting to Build

Here are some tips for starting to build.
• Read the construction steps and relevant techniques sections several times before you begin, so you can plan your method of building and prepare your tools.
• If you alter the plans, remember that one change will necessitate others: in construction steps, tools, and materials needed.
• Get kiln-dried wood whenever possible. It is less likely to warp and is the easiest to work with.
• Mark the wood with a pencil, and account for the width of the saw kerf while measuring.
• Acurate measuring and cutting are critical and should never be rushed. It's a good idea to double-check all your measurements. You can always cut a board shorter, but you can't make it longer.

Then proceed with patience and care. Building a project as a labor of love naturally ensures it of a long and useful life.

The project process chart on the accompanying page gives the major steps involved in the projects. (We have omitted measuring, simple nailing and screwing, insetting hinges, and finishing.) This will tell you at a glance what techniques are used in each project and should help you plan where to begin. Then familiarize yourself with the construction steps for your project, study the illustrations carefully, read the techniques section, and take up your tools.

PROJECT PROGRESS CHART

	Straight sawing	Curved sawing	Angled sawing	Mitered corners	Special shaping	Drilling/bolts	Gluing/nailing	Gluing/screwing	Gluing/clamping	Gluing/drilling/dowel joints	Countersinking/plugging	Mortise/tenon	Dadoes/notches	Shaping edges	Rabbets	Plastic laminate
KITCHEN																
Round cutting board	●	●	●					●								
Rectangular cutting board	●							●	●							
Knife holder	●							●				●				
Lattice trivet												●				
Dowel trivet	●											●		●		
Cookbook holder	●		●										●			
Bed table	●								●			●		●		
Sawbuck table	●	●			●						●	●				
Kitchen table	●	●				●			●	●		●	●			●
Kitchen island	●				●		●		●	●		●	●	●		
Wine rack	●								●							
Roll-out drawers	●						●		●			●				
End-of-cabinet shelves	●						●					●				
Pot and pan rack	●				●							●				
Dish rack	●							●				●				
LIVING/DINING																
Bookcase lamp				●		●										
Globe lamp	●						●				●					
Shoji lamp	●						●							●		
Magazine rack	●									●		●				
Firewood tower	●									●		●				
Display boxes	●						●							●		
Folding screen	●								●							
Mirror frame	●			●				●		●			●	●		
Glass-top tables	●								●			●				
Coffee table	●						●		●			●				
Oak parson's table	●					●		●		●						
Modular unit chest	●					●		●	●				●			
Modular pedestals	●			●		●										
Sandwich drawers	●					●						●	●			
Book/display case	●					●			●							
DESKS/STORAGE																
Hanging desk	●			●		●						●		●		
Wall-phone desk	●					●						●		●		
Filing cabinet desk	●					●										●
Cubbyhole case	●					●						●				
Corner desk	●			●		●								●	●	
Sandwich desk	●			●		●						●		●		
Sports storage	●					●										
Bathroom storage	●					●			●			●				
Cellar wine rack	●	●			●				●			●				
Cedar chest	●	●	●					●	●	●				●		
Children's center	●				●	●					●		●		●	
CHILDREN'S FURNITURE/TOYS																
Blocks	●													●		
Coat rack																
Bulletin board				●		●										
Easel	●				●	●	●							●		
Doll house	●			●		●									●	
Toy chest	●					●										
Teeter totter	●	●				●	●					●		●	●	
Child's bed	●											●		●		
Rocking horse	●	●	●		●	●						●		●	●	

From simple trivets, chopping blocks or dish racks to more complex items like tables, cabinet storage units, or a kitchen island, here is a storehouse of practical and beautiful projects for your kitchen.

The kitchen is a wonderful location for the natural warmth and beauty of wood and the special appeal of something made by hand. In fact, the kitchen is a storehouse of woodworking opportunities. From a simple cutting board to a full-size table, almost anything you make for your kitchen will be used over and over again, providing daily enjoyment for everyone. Projects like the Kitchen Island invite family and friends to gather 'round and work together.

Our kitchen projects are not only practical, but some are strikingly beautiful. And if you are a beginning woodworker, these are good projects for learning the basic woodworking processes, since the book's major construction techniques are covered by them.

But beginner or not, these are fun projects and provide a great opportunity for experimenting and for sharpening your skills. For example, the round cutting board needn't be round. You can cut free-form shapes of various sizes, and combine different woods to assess their effect. You can experiment with joints and finishes, and use your growing skills on other, more complex items.

There are excellent ideas here for solving space problems. End-of-cabinet shelves can be used almost anywhere, embellished with fine molding. The roll-out drawers can be used to create a complete storage unit for baking supplies or utensils. They may even stir your

imagination to create other affordable changes in your cupboards. If our pot and pan rack doesn't quite suit your needs, alter the design so it can be hung from the ceiling.

All of our projects are designed to be altered, although if you follow them exactly you needn't do any planning because we've done it for you. But if you do want to make your own plans, use the roll-out drawers for a model, whether you build them or not. Since they must be built to fit in your cupboards, we explain the steps we took to plan our drawer dimensions and calculate the lumber we needed. Our thinking aloud may help you plan any project.

Many of the kitchen projects are small in scale, making them immediately approachable and providing instant satisfaction. The lattice trivet is a wonderful project for trying out that new router you got for Christmas, or for experimenting with exotic woods. Since you need so little wood, the cost is small but the effect is very striking.

The sawbuck table was designed to be made with hand tools if you are interested in traditional woodworking craftsmanship. Or you can use power tools to make the same cuts. Either way will result in a beautiful table that you will be proud to use and to show off.

CUTTING BOARDS

These will draw so many compliments, you may not want to admit how easy they are to build. The sizes of both may be varied, as well as your choices of wood. Cutting boards make welcome, attractive gifts, and are perfect uses for scrap lumber. A lustrous, safe finish is provided by mineral oil.

ROUND CUTTING BOARD CONSTRUCTION

Step 1. Mill the wood scraps to approximate size and sand the 2-inch surfaces to be glued so they are smooth and even.

Step 2. Stack all the pieces side-by-side in an attractive pattern of light and dark bands, with the best edges forming the upper surface.

Step 3. Glue and clamp all the pieces together (see page 90) and set aside to dry overnight.

Step 4. When the glue is dry, plane both sides smooth (see page 93).

Step 5. Draw a circle with a pencil compass or a plate—or have fun with a free-form shape.

Step 6. Set the saw blade at about a 10-degree angle. The best side of the board should be up when you cut, and the bottom should be smaller than the top.

Step 7. Cut a flat area on one side of the board, perpendicular to the direction of the glue joints. How far into the circle you cut is up to to you; we cut 1½ inches into the circle, making the flat side about 7¾ inches wide.

Step 8. Round over the top edge and sand any blemishes on the side before attaching the handle.

Step 9. Drill a 1-inch hole perpendicular to the flat side to accept the handle. The hole should be angled downward slightly to give the handle an upward angle.

Step 10. Fit the handle and determine its finished length. (Ours is 8½ inches.) Then remove it, cut it to length, and round over the edge with sandpaper.

Step 11. Glue the end of the dowel and tap it into place.

Step 12. Hammer the rubber bumper tacks into the bottom, spacing them evenly about ¾ inch from the edge.

Step 13. Sand well and rub with mineral oil.

LUMBER TO BUY	MILL TO	FOR PROJECT PIECE
Walnut and cherry scraps		**Round cutting board**
1×2s, 2×2s	many 2″×15″ pieces	Total width: 15″
Maple dowel		
1 1″dia.×1′	1 1″ dia.×8½″	Handle
Oak (FAS grade)		**Rectangular cutting board**
1 2″×8″×2′	1 1¾″×7¼″×16″	Center
Walnut (FAS grade)		
1 2″×4″×6′	2 1¾″×3½″×24″	Sides
	2 1¾″×3½″×8″	

Hardware & Miscellaneous: Round Cutting Board	
1	large brass screw eye (or leather thong)
4	rubber bumper tacks
	Glue

Hardware & Miscellaneous: Rectangular Cutting Board	
24	⅜″×2″ grooved dowels
	Glue

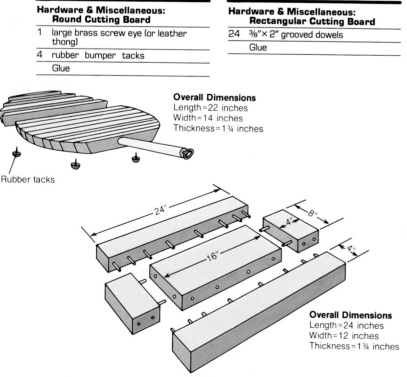

Rubber tacks

Overall Dimensions
Length=22 inches
Width=14 inches
Thickness=1¾ inches

24″

16″

8″

4″

4″

Overall Dimensions
Length=24 inches
Width=12 inches
Thickness=1¾ inches

RECTANGULAR CUTTING BOARD CONSTRUCTION

Step 1. Mill the lumber. You can use different dimensions than those given here, but the two smaller pieces of walnut must be cut to the width of the oak center-piece.

Step 2. Set the pieces together as they will be glued and mark where the dowels will be inserted. Drill the dowel holes. (See page 89.)

Step 3. Apply glue to all the pieces and the dowels, tap them together with a rubber mallet, and clamp all the joints. If you're short on clamps this may be done in stages, first gluing the small ends to the center blocks, and later the sides.

Step 4. When the glue is dry, plane both sides smooth (see page 93).

Step 5. Sand all the surfaces and edges and finish with mineral oil.

KNIFE HOLDER

This easily made knife block is a simple, beginning project that you are unlikely to find in a store, and an attractive accent to a kitchen. By installing it under a countertop it is handy for the cook, yet away from the reach of small children. And it makes an excellent gift. Choose a wood to match or complement your kitchen or that of a friend.

KNIFE HOLDER CONSTRUCTION

Step 1. Cut two pieces of wood, each 20 inches long.

Step 2. Mark one of the boards to fit your knives. If you are making this as a gift, we suggest marking three 1-inch slots and one each of 1½, 1¾, 2, and 2⅛ inches. The slot for the sharpening steel should be ⅝-inch wide.

Step 3. Use a dado set to make the slots, cutting all but three ⅛-inch deep. The slots for the two widest knives should be ³⁄₁₆-inch deep, and the slot for the steel ⁵⁄₁₆-inch deep.

Step 4. Hold the two boards together and mark the steel slot on the uncut board. Cut that ⁵⁄₁₆-inch deep as well, so when the two boards are joined the steel slot will be a ⅝-inch square.

Step 5. Glue and clamp or screw the boards together, and remove excess glue.

Step 6. When the glue is dry, clean, sand, and finish the block.

Step 7. Mount it with screws from the inside of a cabinet or counter. If your countertop has an overhang, use pieces of matching lumber to shim the holder, allowing access to the slots. (See illustration.)

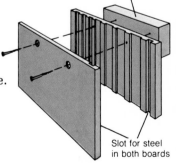

Shim (width depends on amount of overhang. See Step 7)

Slot for steel in both boards

Overall Dimensions
Length = 20 inches
Width = 1⅛ inches (without shim)
Thickness = 11½ inches

MATERIALS TO BUY	
1	1"× 12"× 2' walnut (FAS grade)
6	1¼"× #8 wood screws (optional)
	Glue

TRIVETS

Can you spare an hour for a trivet? Here are two more good reasons to make one today: it will always be useful and makes a wonderful gift. Our lattice trivet was made from a small piece of brilliant-red "vermilion" wood, and the dowel trivet from leftover walnut and dowels. Each took an hour to make, from start to finish.

MATERIALS TO BUY

Lattice trivet

1	1"×10"×10" Andaman padouk (vermilion wood)

Dowel trivet

1	2"×2"×26" walnut (FAS grade)
3	Maple or birch dowels ⅝" dia.×4'
	Glue

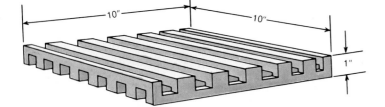

LATTICE TRIVET CONSTRUCTION

Step 1. Decide how wide you want the grooves in your trivet and how much wood you want between them, and then mark the grooves on the edge of the wood. Our lattice is symmetrical— ⅝-inch grooves with ⅝ inches between them—but with a bit of creativity an infinite number of patterns are possible.

Step 2. Set the dado attachment to cut the width you want. The height of the blades must be set to cut away only a little more than half the thickness of the wood. Cut the grooves on one side.

Step 3. Turn the piece over, rotate it 90 degrees, and cut the same pattern again.

Step 4. Sand the trivet carefully and finish it as desired. We rubbed ours with nontoxic mineral oil.

DOWEL TRIVET CONSTRUCTION

Step 1. Cut the dowel into 12 pieces 12 inches long.

Step 2. Run a rabbet ¾ inch by ¾ inch the length of the walnut.

Step 3. Cut a ½-inch round finger-groove in the underside of the rabbet, using a router with a core-box bit and an edge guide. Then cut the length in half, making two handles.

Step 4. Mark the horizontal center-line for the dowels ⅝ inch below the top on the inside face of each handle. The center point for each dowel should be marked at 1-inch intervals on the horizontal center-line, starting 1 inch from each end.

Step 5. Drill a hole ⅝-inch wide and ½-inch deep at each of the center points. (See page 89 for marking depth.) Sand each handle.

Step 6. To assemble the trivet, put glue into the end holes on each handle and tap the 12 dowels into one handle. Set the other handle on the ends of the dowels and guide each dowel into its hole, in turn, from one end to the other. Use a mallet to tap the dowels into place, then remove excess glue and allow it to set.

Step 7. Sand and finish as you wish.

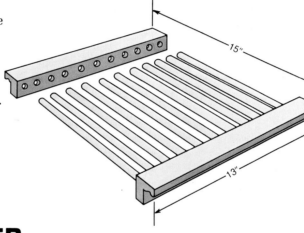

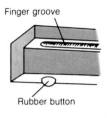

Finger groove

Rubber button

COOKBOOK HOLDER

Make two parallel saw kerfs in a piece of wood, insert two sheets of plastic, and voila!—you have a holder that will keep your cookbook open and protect it from spatters while you work. You can make this of scrap lumber, or dress it up by using fine hardwood or by laminating strips of different kinds of wood.

CONSTRUCTION

Step 1. Set the saw blade to a 30-degree angle and rip the two saw kerfs to a depth of ½ to ¾ inch. The first kerf should be about 3 inches from the front, the second 2½ inches behind it.

Step 2. Shape the block of wood as you wish, and shape the top edge with a router.

Step 3. Sand smooth and finish as desired (see page 93).

Step 4. Insert the two plastic sheets in the kerfs.

MATERIALS TO BUY

1	2" × 12" × 20" cherry or scrap
2	⅛" × 12" × 20" acrylic sheets

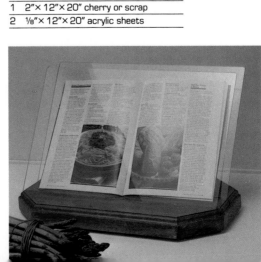

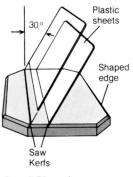

30°

Plastic sheets

Shaped edge

Saw Kerfs

Overall Dimensions
Length = 20 inches
Width = 12 inches
Height = 11¾ inches

BED TABLE

Build this as a treat to yourself and to someone you love. For you, it's a treat because it's so easy to make. And for a loved one, getting a meal in bed is a wonderful gift—especially on so well-designed and attractive a table. The separate tray allows you to position the base before setting down spillable liquids.

CONSTRUCTION

Step 1. Mill the 2 by 2s to the sizes indicated.

Step 2. Assemble the base with glue and dowels as illustrated. (See page 89 for doweling instructions.) Clamp it and set it aside to dry.

Step 3. Make a rabbet ⅝-inch wide by ⅞-inch deep in what will be the bottom inside edge of the four tray pieces.

Step 4. Dado a slot ¼-inch deep by ¼-inch wide and ¼ inch below the top inside edge of all four tray pieces to accept the plywood insert.

Step 5. Rabbet the two tray side-pieces ⅞-inch deep to accept the ends of the front and back.

Step 6. Chamfer the inside edge above the ¼-inch groove on all tray side-pieces (see page 88). Stop the chamfer about 1 inch from each end of the front and back pieces so it doesn't intrude on the end joint.

Step 7. Set the pieces together on your workbench and measure between the insides of the ¼-inch grooves to check for the correct size of the plywood tray. Then cut the ¼-inch plywood to size. If all your cutting has been accurate the plywood can be cut to the dimensions we gave; if not, make the necessary adjustments.

Step 8. Assemble the tray by gluing and doweling the sides with the plywood insert in place. There is no need to glue the insert, as it is held snugly on all sides. Clamp the tray and set it aside to dry.

Step 9. When all the glue joints are dry, clean and sand the table and finish as desired.

LUMBER TO BUY	MILL TO		FOR PROJECT PIECE
Cherry (FAS grade)			
3 2″× 2″× 6′	4	1¾″× 1¾″× 12″	Base
	4	1¾″× 1¾″× 12¼″	
	2	1¾″× 1¾″× 18½″	
	2	1¾″× 1¾″× 18″	Tray
	2	1¾″× 1¾″× 22½″	
Cherry plywood			
1 ¼″× 18″× 24″	1	¼″× 21½″× 15¼″	Insert

Hardware & Miscellaneous	
32	⅜″ dia.× 1½″ grooved dowels
	Glue

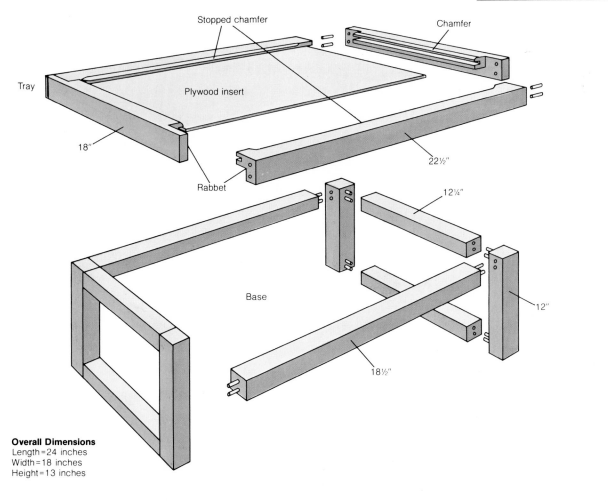

Stopped chamfer

Chamfer

Tray

Plywood insert

18″

Rabbet

22½″

12¼″

12″

Base

18½″

Overall Dimensions
Length = 24 inches
Width = 18 inches
Height = 13 inches

SAWBUCK TABLE

This type of traditional American folk table has been used since the days of the early settlers, who valued its simplicity, natural beauty, and grace. They built it with softwood and hand tools, without the two braces—which we added for greater stability. This makes a good work table for a large kitchen, or an informal dining table for indoor or outdoor use.

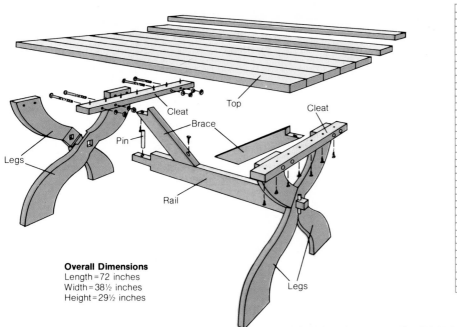

Overall Dimensions
Length = 72 inches
Width = 38½ inches
Height = 29½ inches

1-inch squares

CONSTRUCTION

Step 1. To make the tabletop, straighten the edges of the 2 by 6 boards if necessary and glue them together. (See page 89 for joining methods.) If you wish, you may chamfer the edges of each board (see page 88) to make a small v-groove where they join.

Step 2. Draw the leg pattern on 1-inch-square grid paper, then transfer the pattern to the four 2 by 10s. Cut out the legs with a band or saber saw.

Step 3. Couple each pair of legs and carefully mark the edges of the cross-lap joints. Notch each to half the depth of the leg (see page 90). Mark each pair so they don't get mixed up.

Step 4. Cut a 1½- by 1½-inch mortise in each coupled leg for the rail tenon, using a drill and chisel.

Step 5. Cut a tenon 1½ by 1½ by 5 inches on each end of the rail by making repeated passes with a saw.

Step 6. Insert the rail tenons into the leg mortises and mark the position for each dowel pin.

Step 7. Drill a ⅝-inch hole for each dowel pin about 1/32 inch over the mark so the pins will bind tightly against the legs.

Step 8. Assemble the rail and legs and drive the dowel pins into place.

Step 9. Lay the tabletop upside down on your workbench after the glue has dried. Screw the 2- by 4-inch cleats to the underside; the measurement between them should be 45½ inches—the distance between the outer sides of the legs. Set the leg/rail assembly upside down on the tabletop so the top of the legs rest on the table and against the cleats.

Step 10 (optional). If you choose to use braces, they should be measured and cut at this stage. As illustrated, cut a notch 1½ by 3½ inches at a 45-degree angle in one end of each brace so they fit against the cleats. Hold each brace in place on a cleat and mark the other end where it intersects the rail; then cut it off.

Step 11. Drill two ¼-inch holes through the top of each leg and the cleats where they join. Connect them with carriage bolts.

Step 12 (optional). Screw the braces in position between the cleat and the rail.

Step 13. Sand everything smooth—especially the top—and finish as desired (see page 93).

LUMBER TO BUY		MILL TO	FOR PROJECT PIECE
Inland red cedar			
7	2″ × 6″ × 6′	Straighten edges	Top
4	2″ × 10″ × 4′	Follow pattern	Legs
2	2″ × 4″ × 8′	2 1½″ × 3½″ × 30″	Cleats
		1 1½″ × 3½″ × 52″	Rail
		2 1½″ × 3½″ × 18″	Braces (optional)
Dowel			
1	⅝″ dia. × 1′	2 ⅝″ dia. × 6″	Pins

Hardware & Miscellaneous	
8	¼″ × 6″ carriage bolts; washers; nuts
18	2½″ × #10 flat-head wood screws
	Glue

KITCHEN TABLE

This was designed as a family table, and several features make it really quite special. It has obvious grace, yet the strength to withstand many years—perhaps generations—of use, and is remarkably easy to build. Choose a beautiful wood, follow the step-by-step instructions, and before you know it this beautiful table will be standing before you.

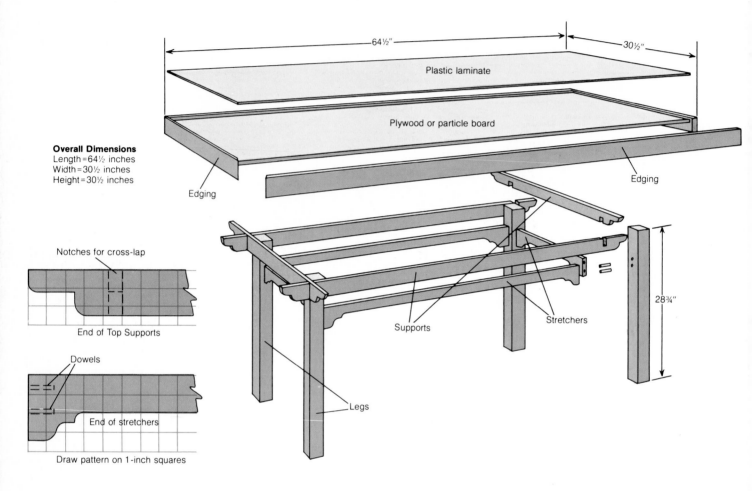

Overall Dimensions
Length = 64½ inches
Width = 30½ inches
Height = 30½ inches

CONSTRUCTION

Step 1. Mill all the lumber, mitering the ends of the top edging at 45 degrees.

Step 2. Follow the diagram and mark the detailing on the top supports and stretchers. Cut the detailing with a coping or saber saw, and notch the top supports for the cross-lap joints (see page 87).

Step 3. Round over the outside bottom edge of the top supports and the four long edges of the stretchers (see page 88).

Step 4. Sand all the pieces.

Step 5. Mark the position of the stretchers on the legs. The tops of the stretchers are 6½ inches below the tabletop and centered on the sides of the legs. Drill holes for two dowels in the end of each stretcher and in the legs where they join (see page 89).

Step 6. Mark the top supports where they join the tops of the legs, and then drill ³⁄₃₂-inch pilot holes and ½-inch counterbores for screws and plugs (see page 89).

Step 7. Dowel, glue, and clamp the stretchers between the four legs.

Step 8. Immediately after placing the stretchers, assemble the top supports with their edge cross-laps, and glue and screw them to the legs through the pilot holes you made in step 6. Check all the joints with a framing square and adjust the clamps if necessary.

Step 9. Cement the plastic laminate to the top and press it firmly until it sets. Then trim the edges flush (see page 92).

Step 10. Glue and nail the top edging to the plywood or particle board flush with the top surface of the plastic laminate. Conceal the nails and fill the holes (see page 93).

Step 11. When the glue is dry, secure the top to the inside of the top supports with the chair braces.

Step 12. Finish the table as desired.

MATERIALS TO BUY		MILL TO		FOR PROJECT PIECE
Ash (FAS grade)				
2	3″× 3″× 5′	4	2½″× 2½″× 28¾″	Legs
4	1″× 3″× 8′	2	¾″× 2½″× 64½″	Top edging
		2	¾″× 2½″× 30½″	
		2	¾″× 2½″× 51″	Top supports
		2	¾″× 2½″× 23″	
2	1″× 4″× 10′	2	¾″× 3½″× 36″	Stretchers
		2	¾″× 3½″× 14″	
Plywood or particle board				
1	¾″× 4′× 8′	1	¾″× 29″× 63″	Top
Plastic laminate (Formica, etc.)				
1	3′× 6′			Top
Dowel				
1	½″dia.× 1′	16	½″dia.× ½″	Dowel plugs

Hardware & Miscellaneous		
16	⅜″ dia.× 2½″ grooved dowels	Contact cement
16	1½″× #10 flat-head wood screws	Wood putty
8	2″ chair braces with ¾″ screws	Glue
4d	finishing nails	

KITCHEN ISLAND

This will give your kitchen a new focal point, and enough counter space to prepare your scrumptious meals—even to invite your family or friends to help you prepare them. And the shelf and drawers place your cannisters and tools within easy reach. You'll need a 7- by 8-foot empty floor area to allow at least 30 inches between the island and surrounding appliances and cabinets.

CONSTRUCTION

Step 1. Mill the pieces of lumber to size. To make your work look more professional, cut the skirt pieces and drawer front for each side, in order, from the same piece of wood, so the grain matches from piece to piece.

Step 2. The legs can be left straight, or you can use a tapering jig on the two exterior sides—making them 3½ inches wide at the top and 2¾ inches wide at the bottom (see page 88). In either case, round over the corners of the legs from the bottom to a point 6½ inches from the top.

Step 3. Cut a 45-degree flat area 1½ inches across the top inside corner of each leg, extending 5 inches from the

top. An easy way to do this is to tack two 45-degree blocks to the sides of the leg to hold the corner up, and make repeat passes with a saw. Screw a stud bolt into the middle of the flat area about 2 inches from the top (see page 89).

Step 4. Assemble the skirt-base frame with glue and dowels (see page 89), making sure you square and center the sides when you mark the dowel holes and when you clamp the frame. Set aside to dry.

Step 5. Glue and screw the skirt pieces in place on the skirt-base frame. The skirt should be flush with the base at the ends and centered on the base at the sides. (This leaves a small lip on the inside of the frame for later attachment of drawer guides.) Glue in the corner blocks, using small nails if necessary to hold them in place. Set aside to dry.

Step 6. Screw the skirt to the chopping-block top after turning them both upside down and positioning the skirt so the base frame is flush with one end of the chopping block, and centered from side to side. Make pilot holes and then insert screws at an angle from the inside of the skirt into the bottom of the chopping block.

Step 7. Attach the legs by setting each in its approximate position on the upside-down top. Mark where the stud bolts meet the corner blocks, then drill a ¼-inch hole at each of these marks and insert the stud bolts. Secure these with washers and nuts, and wiggle the leg a bit as you tighten each nut to be sure it nests snugly against the skirt. Turn the table upright.

Step 8. To assemble the shelf rail, dado the lap joints where the 8-inch vertical supports cross the 25½-inch piece— about 5 inches from each end. Glue and nail the 11-inch pieces to the ends of the 25½-inch rail, using 6-penny finishing nails.

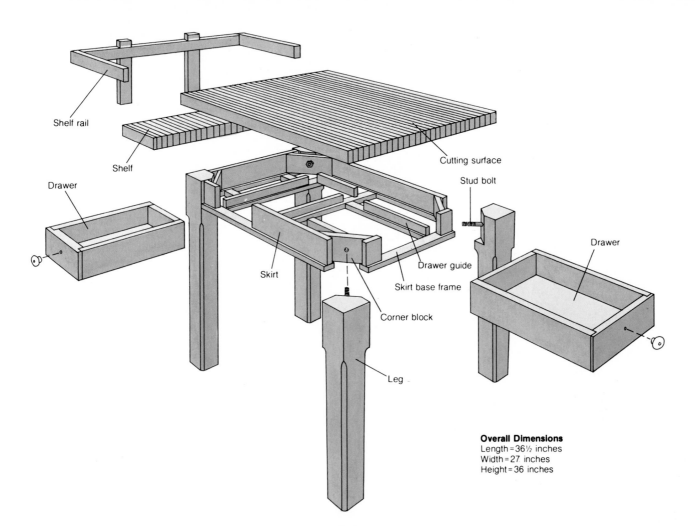

Shelf rail

Shelf

Drawer

Cutting surface

Stud bolt

Drawer

Skirt

Drawer guide

Skirt base frame

Corner block

Leg

Overall Dimensions
Length = 36½ inches
Width = 27 inches
Height = 36 inches

Step 9. Glue and screw the vertical supports to the chopping block shelf, letting them extend ½ inch below the shelf. Countersink and cover the screws with glued-on dowel caps.

Step 10. Attach the shelf and rail to the island. Insert two screws through each side rail into the side of the top and two screws, toe-nail fashion, through the bottom of the shelf into the legs. Drill pilot holes for all screws. Countersink and cap all visible screws.

Step 11. Build the drawers following one of the methods noted on pages 91-92. Make sure to position the drawer fronts so the grain matches the skirts. The 12-inch-wide drawer should be 14 inches long, and the 8-inch drawer 19 inches long.

Step 12. Nail or screw 1 by 2 scraps to the top of the base frame for drawer guides and stops. The drawers should close flush with the skirt.

Step 13. Remove excess glue and sand thoroughly, then finish as desired. (Leave the top unfinished, or use non-toxic mineral oil.)

LUMBER TO BUY		MILL TO		FOR PROJECT PIECE
Pine (grade B select)				
2	1″× 4″× 6′	1	¾″× 3½″× 21¾″	Skirt and drawer fronts
		1	¾″× 3½″× 16″	
		2	¾″× 3½″× 12″	
		1	¾″× 3½″× 7¾″	
		3	¾″× 3½″× 2″	
5	1″× 2″× 8′	2	¾″× 1½″× 16″	Skirt-base frame
		2	¾″× 1½″× 21¾″	
		2	¾″× 1½″× 19″	
		2	¾″× 1½″× 13½″	
		2	¾″× 1½″× 3½″	
		1	¾″× 1½″× 25½″	Shelf rail
		2	¾″× 1½″× 8″	
		2	¾″× 1½″× 11″	
1	½″× 4″× 8′	2	½″× 3½″× 13¾″	Drawer sides and backs
		1	½″× 3½″× 11″	
		2	½″× 3½″× 18¾″	
		1	½″× 3½″× 6¾″	
2	4″× 4″× 6′	4	3½″× 3½″× 34½″	Legs
Maple chopping block (ready made)				
1	1½″× 25½″× 36″	1	1½″× 25½″× 30″	Cutting surface
Fir plywood				
1	⅛″× 24″× 24″	1	⅛″× 11½″× 18¾″	Drawer bottoms
		1	⅛″× 6¼″× 13¾″	

Hardware & Miscellaneous				
4	¼″× 3″ stud bolts; washers; nuts		2	drawer pulls
34	1¾″× #8 flat-head wood screws		6d	finishing nails
6	⅜″ dowel plugs			Glue

WINE RACK

When you finish this project you'll be richer and wiser: richer by a lovely, well-proportioned rack you can be proud to put into your living room—and, one that holds 18 bottles of wine; and wiser for the skills you'll have learned in measuring and joinery. An advanced beginner can do this quite well—in fact, it's a good ego-builder.

CONSTRUCTION

Step 1. Mill all stock.

Step 2. Draw the lattice pattern on butcher paper as shown in the illustration. The lattice must be centered on a 24½-inch width (the measurement to the inside of the groove in the sides) and positioned vertically to rest on the center of the bottom joints. The lattice boards should be 5½ inches on center—that is, there should be 3¾ inches between boards.

Step 3. Lay the pieces for each of the two lattices on your pattern and carefully mark them where they cross.

Step 4. Dado a notch exactly halfway through the lattice boards where they cross, so they'll be flush when fitted together.

Step 5. Fit each lattice together to be sure all the joints fit. When they do, glue each joint and lay the lattice on a flat surface. Then place heavy material on top of it to apply pressure (such as a sheet of ¾-inch plywood) and let it dry overnight.

Step 6. Dado a groove in the vertical side and bottom pieces to house the lattice. Each groove should be centered and cut to a width of ¾ inch and a depth of ½ inch.

Step 7. Dado a notch in the vertical sides to house the bottoms. The notch should be 3 inches from the bottom, ½-inch deep, and exactly the width of the bottom pieces.

Step 8. Drill ⅜-inch holes 1¼ inches deep in the horizonal and vertical side pieces as shown. Dowel, glue, and clamp them together.

Step 9. Glue and clamp the two bottom pieces between the sides, checking to be sure all the joints are square. Allow to dry overnight.

Step 10. Measure the width for each lattice from groove to groove at both top and bottom. (All four measurements should be 24½ inches, but if they're not

LUMBER TO BUY	MILL TO			FOR PROJECT PIECE
Walnut (FAS grade)				
8 1"× 2"× 6'	4	¾"× 1¾"× 16"		Lattices
	4	¾"× 1¾"× 27"		
	4	¾"× 1¾"× 38"		
	4	¾"× 1¾"× 32"		
	4	¾"× 1¾"× 21"		
	4	¾"× 1¾"× 10"		
	2	¾"× 1¾"× 8⅜"		Caps
3 2"× 3"× 6'	4	1¾"× 2⅞"× 34"		Vertical sides
	2	1¾"× 2⅞"× 24½"		Bottoms
	4	1¾"× 1¾"× 2⅝"		Horizontal sides

Hardware & Miscellaneous	
16	⅜" dia.× 2½" grooved dowels
	Glue

you can make adjustments when you mark and trim the lattices.)

Step 11. Mark the trim measurements on the lattices. Use the center line as your guide to make sure you trim the same amount of lattice on each side. Also, mark the trim line for the bottom through the centers of the bottom lattice-joints, as illustrated.

Step 12. Recheck the measurements. A lot of work and wood are wasted if the lattices are cut too small. Then trim the lattices with a hand saw.

Step 13. Remove excess glue with a chisel or scraper and sand all but the caps. (This is harder to do when the rack is assembled.)

Step 14. Slide the lattices into place. They should fit snugly so no gluing or nailing is necessary. If they are loose, squeeze a little glue in the grooves where the lattice touches.

Step 15. Drill four ⅜-inch holes 1¼ inches deep in the caps and tops of the vertical side pieces, and dowel and glue the caps on top of each side.

Step 16. Clean and sand the caps and the joints around them, and oil or finish the rack as you wish (see page 94).

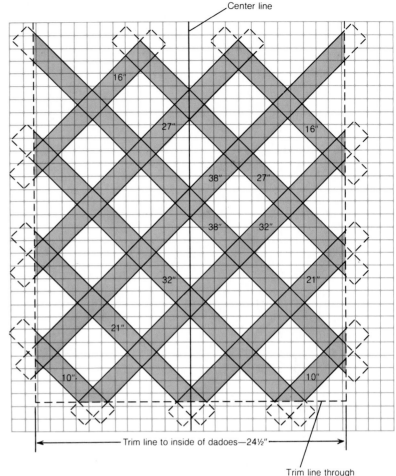

Center line

16″
27″
16″
38″   27″
38″   32″
32″   21″
21″
10″   10″

Trim line to inside of dadoes—24½″

Trim line through center of bottom joints

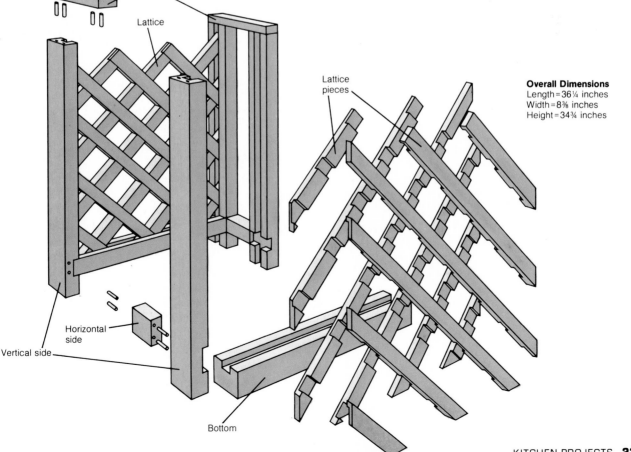

Caps

Lattice

Lattice pieces

Overall Dimensions
Length = 36¼ inches
Width = 8⅜ inches
Height = 34¾ inches

Horizontal side

Vertical side

Bottom

ROLL-OUT DRAWERS

This is one solution to some kitchen problems, and it beats expensive remodeling. By building simple roll-out shelves you can convert a small part of your kitchen into a high-intensity, special-use area best suited to your needs. Just take the space of one cupboard, decide what you need, and follow the steps we took to arrive at our dimensions.

DESIGNING

Step 1. Decide where you want the roll-outs and remove any existing shelves.

Step 2. Carefully measure the depth of the cabinet and the height and width of the opening. Our cabinet is 20 inches deep, but a 1-inch BX electric cable runs up the back so the drawers can be only 19 inches deep. Our opening is 19⅜ inches wide, but the drawers must be 1 inch narrower to leave room for drawer slides. The height of the opening is 27⅜ inches.

Step 3. Decide how many drawers you want to fit in this space and what you want to store in them. We needed a place for knives and other long kitchen tools and small appliances. We also wanted a place to store onions, potatoes, and other bulky produce that needs to be kept in a cool dry place.

After thinking through several options, we decided to make the top drawer 3½ inches high with slots for knives and compartments for other long tools, and the bottom drawer about 7 inches high with big square compartments for produce; and to use the rest of the space in the middle—about 16 inches high—for a shallow platform-drawer to hold the food processor, mixer, blender, and other small appliances.

Step 4. Make a materials list. As the drawers are to be about 3½ inches high and 7 inches high, it is easiest to use 4-inch and 8-inch stock. The width and depth of the drawers tell us how much we need of each. (We always buy a little more lumber than we really need because we do make mistakes, and we can always use the scraps for something.)

CONSTRUCTION

Step 1. Mill all the pine to the sizes shown, and make a separate pile of pieces for each drawer and for the knife slots.

Step 2. Glue three of the four knife-slot pieces together like a sandwich. Clamp and set them aside.

Step 3. Prepare the pieces and construct the drawers as described in the technique section (see page 91). Before you assemble the pieces, dado the slots in the fronts, backs, and sides to accept the dividers, and cut the "handles" in the drawer fronts as you want them. Make sure the knife-drawer cut out is deep enough to accommodate your knife handles.

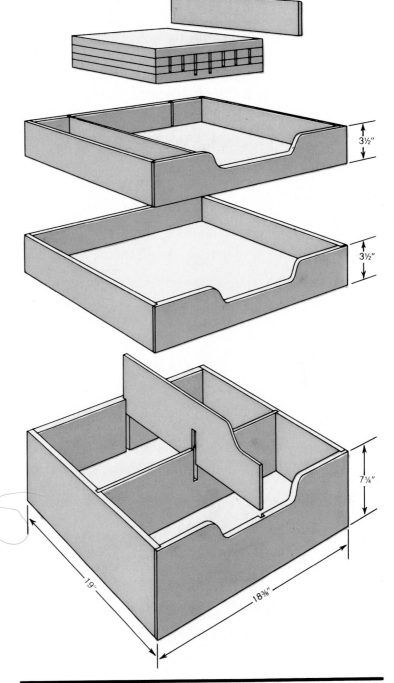

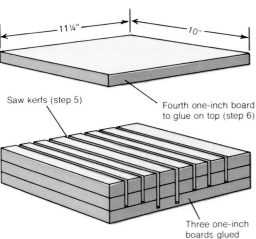

Saw kerfs (step 5)

Fourth one-inch board to glue on top (step 6)

Three one-inch boards glued together (step 2)

Step 4. Insert the dividers. The ones that cross will have to be marked and a slot cut halfway through them so they will interlock.

Step 5. When the glue is dry on the knife holder, make the slots by sawing through the top two pieces about 1 inch apart. If you have one or two very wide and thick-bladed knives, you should make deeper slots and widen them a little with an extra pass of the saw.

Step 6. Glue the fourth knife-slot piece on top of the sandwich, clamp it, and let it dry.

Step 7. Use two screws to attach the knife holder to the drawer, placing them carefully to miss the slots.

Step 8. Mark the position of the drawer slides in the inside of the cabinet, and shim the excess space so the sides are flush with the opening.

Step 9. Fasten the slide channels to the inside of the cabinet and to the drawers per manufacturer instructions.

Step 10. Fit the drawers and adjust accordingly.

Step 11. Sand and finish the drawers as you wish.

LUMBER TO BUY		MILL TO		FOR PROJECT PIECE
Pine (grade B select)				
1	1"× 4"× 4'	2	¾"× 3½"× 18⅜"	Fronts
2	½"× 4"× 6'	4	½"× 3½"× 18¾"	Sides
		2	½"× 3½"× 17⅜"	Backs
1	1"× 8"× 2'	1	¾"× 7¼"× 18⅜"	Front
1	½"× 8"× 6'	2	½"× 7¼"× 18¾"	Sides
		1	½"× 7¼"× 17⅜"	Back
1	1"× 12"× 4'	4	¾"× 11¼"× 10"	Knife slots
Fir plywood (grade AD)				
1	¼"× 4'× 8'	3	¼"× 17¾"× 18½"	Bottoms
		2	¼"× 3"× 18¼"	Top drawer dividers
		1	¼"× 6¾"× 18¼"	Bottom drawer dividers
		1	¼"× 6¾"× 17¾"	

Hardware & Miscellaneous	
3 pair 18" extension drawer slides	¾"× #6 flat-head wood screws (2)
4d finishing nails	Glue

END-OF-CABINET SHELVES

Here's another simple, attractive project to make better use of space. The bare end of a cabinet is the perfect place for spices, pretty plates, and things to keep at hand. These shelves blend in with almost any style of kitchen, especially with complementary molding. And with matching wood or finish they won't look added on.

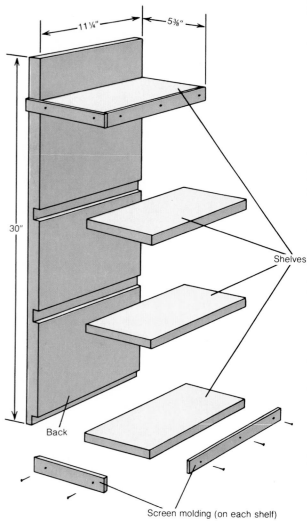

LUMBER TO BUY	MILL TO			FOR PROJECT PIECE
Pine (grade B select)				
1	1"× 12"× 4'	1	¾"× 11¼"× 30"	Back
1	½"× 6"× 6'	4	½"× 5½"× 11¼"	Shelves
Screen molding				
1	¼"× ¾"× 6'	4	¼"× ¾"× 11¼"	Shelf lip
		4	¼"× ¾"× 6⅛"	

Hardware & Miscellaneous
⅝" brads
6d finishing nails
Mounting hardware
Glue

CONSTRUCTION

Step 1. Mill all the pieces.

Step 2. Dado four grooves ½-inch wide by ⅜-inch deep across the width of the back. Make the first groove at the bottom, and the other three at 8-inch intervals.

Step 3. Glue and nail the four shelves into the grooves, leaving ¼ inch for a shelf lip on the outside.

Step 4. Glue and nail the shelf lip to the front and side edges of the shelves.

Step 5. Sand and finish to match the existing cabinet.

Step 6. Mount the unit to the cabinet.

POT AND PAN RACK

This is one solution to kitchen space problems, and the rack is convenient, attractive, and easy to build. You can use it to dry herbs and hang vegetables as well as cooking utensils, and it would be perfect mounted near the island shown on page 20.

CONSTRUCTION

Step 1. Mill stock to size.

Step 2. Notch all the pieces, making sure the notches go exactly halfway through the piece and that each is exactly the width of the board it will house. (See page 87 for ways to cut notches.) Label both sides of each joint to make later identification easier. Sand all pieces to prepare them for finishing.

Step 3. Drill bolt holes by holding each joint together and drilling through both pieces at once. Insert and finger-tighten the bolts as you drill each hole.

Step 4. Decide where you want the large and small screw hooks. Drill ⅛- or 1/16-inch pilot holes as needed, and screw the hooks into place.

Step 5. If you want to paint the hardware or the entire unit, it is best to do so before assembling and mounting the unit. Stain and oil or varnish can be used with the hardware in place.

Step 6. Hang the rack carefully with at least two 4-inch lag screws that penetrate the studs, as a rack full of pots and pans is very heavy.

LUMBER TO BUY	MILL TO		FOR PROJECT PIECE
Birch (FAS grade)			
2 2"×4"×6'	2	1¾"×3½"×16"	A
	2	1¾"×3½"×18"	B
	2	1¾"×3½"×30"	C
1 2"×2"×6'	2	1¾"×1¾"×10"	D
	1	1¾"×1¾"×30"	E

Hardware & Miscellaneous			
4	¼"×4" carriage bolts; washers; nuts	20	large screw hooks
		15	small screw hooks
6	¼"×2" carriage bolts; washers; nuts	2	5/16"×4" lag screws

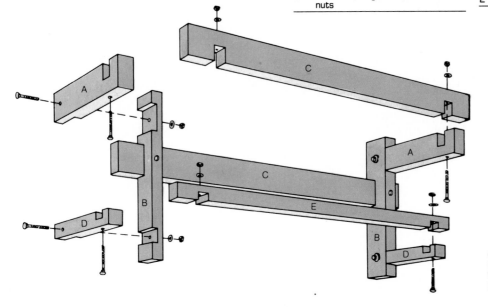

Overall Dimensions
Length = 30 inches
Width = 16 inches
Height = 18 inches

DISH RACK

If you lack cabinet space or have a pretty set of dishes to display, here's one solution. These dimensions fit our dishes and other sets we tried, but some dishes are too thick to fit the space between the dowels. Measure the diameter and thickness of your dishes and then plan your rack. Any hardwood will be attractive, especially one that contrasts with standard birch or maple dowels.

LUMBER TO BUY	MILL TO			FOR PROJECT PIECE
Birch (FAS grade)				
1 1"× 2"× 10'	2	¾"× 1¾"× 11¾"		Ends
	2	¾"× 1¾"× 25"		Sides
	2	¾"× 1¾"× 13"		Wall brackets
	2	⅜"× 1¾"× 2¼"		Bracket projections
1 2"× 2"× 2'	2	1⅛"× 1¾"× 11¾"		Salad-plate sides
Birch or maple dowel				
4 ½" dia.× 4'	9	½" dia.× 10½"		Dinner-plate holders
	9	½" dia.× 8½"		Salad-plate holders

Hardware & Miscellaneous

12	⅜" dia.× 1½" grooved dowels
2'	brass chain
4	brass screw eyes
2	1½"× #8 round-head brass screws; washers
	Glue

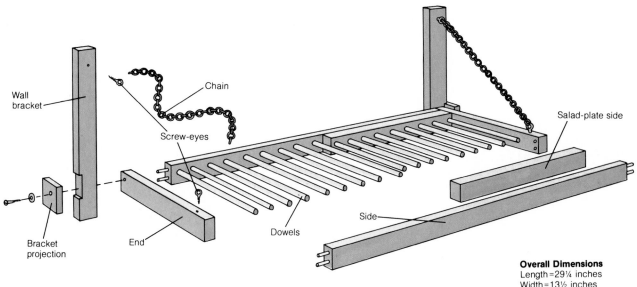

Wall bracket

Chain

Screw-eyes

Salad-plate side

Bracket projection

End

Dowels

Side

Overall Dimensions
Length=29¼ inches
Width=13½ inches
Height=13 inches

CONSTRUCTION

Step 1. Mill all stock.

Step 2. Glue and clamp the salad-plate sides to the inside edge of the full-length sides.

Step 3. Mark the holes for the ½-inch dowels on a line drawn ⅝ inch from the top edge of the sides. Our dinner-plate dowels are 1½ inches apart (center-to-center); the salad-plate dowels are 1⁵⁄₁₆ inches apart.

Step 4. Drill the ½-inch holes to a depth of slightly more than ½-inch deep (see page 89), using a drill press or hole square to keep the holes perpendicular to the surface.

Step 5. Mark and drill the holes for the ⅜-inch dowels that will hold the ends to the sides (see page 89).

Step 6. Connect the dowels and sides by laying one side on your workbench with the holes up and tapping the 8½-inch dowels into the holes. Set the other side on top and, working from one end to the other, insert the dowels into the holes and tap the side into place with a mallet.

Step 7. Dowel, glue, and clamp the ends.

Step 8. Dado a notch in each of the wall brackets to house the bracket projections. Mark the width and depth carefully and cut the notch with repeated saw passes.

Step 9. Glue the projections into place. They can be held with clamps until dry, or secured with small brads.

Step 10. When the glue has dried, sand all of the joints smooth and round over the top outside edges, stopping about 1 inch at the back of each side.

Step 11. Attach the brackets to the rack. Drill a ³⁄₁₆-inch hole in each projection ½ inch from the top and ½ inch from the back of the rack sides. Insert round-head screws and washers through the projections into the sides.

Step 12. Put a screw eye in each bracket about ½ inch from the top, and a screw eye in the top of each side piece about 1½ inches from the front.

Step 13. Hold a square against one bracket and stand it upright at a right angle to the rack. Measure the distance between the screw eyes and cut a piece of chain to fit. Open the screw eyes with pliers, attach the chain, and squeeze the screw eyes together again. Repeat the process for the other side.

Step 14. Clean, sand, and finish the rack.

Step 15. To attach the rack to the wall, drill one or two holes in each bracket and use 2½-inch round-head screws or molly bolts to secure it.

GLASS-TOPPED
COCKTAIL TABLE

WOOD = WALNUT

• LIVING & DINING ROOMS •

Here is a selection of fine tables and accessories for the entertainment centers of your home. The modular units can serve as a room divider or they can be arranged to create a buffet, desk or dresser. The cases and shelves can hold books, records, stereo equipment or just about anything you want.

These projects would compare favorably with anything you could buy in a store—and one of the beauties of building them yourself is that you *couldn't* buy most of them in a store.

Many of the projects in this chapter can be built by beginners, even the ones that look complicated. The glass-top tables are a case in point. Only three construction steps are required: milling the 12 wood pieces to size; joining the legs and skirts with dowels; and routing a square in each leg. What remains is sanding, finishing, and inserting the top. What could be easier?

The real pièce de résistance is the modular unit. To buy anything remotely comparable would cost you a fortune. But perhaps best of all, the modular pieces fit wherever you put them. If you build them for one living space and then move to another, they'll work just as well.

The chest is particularly versatile. You can use one to hold records, others to hold stereo equipment, and others to make a buffet—with panel or glass doors, with or without drawers. You can build them with drawers and stack them as dressers. Or add the sandwich drawer unit to two chests and pedestals to make a wonderful desk (see page 59). Or put them in the middle of a room with the book/display case for a beautiful room divider. Or, or . . . the possibilities are almost limitless.

As for room dividers, the folding screen is

another possibility. You can build this in different sizes and the proportions will hold. Leave it plain, if you like, or add fabric for a different effect; then change the effect by changing the fabric.

For displaying large items, build the book/display section of the modular unit. For smaller items, the 16 display boxes may be just what you need: glue them together and hang them on the wall; stack them; use them individually; these are just some of the possibilities.

The globe lamp and the magazine rack are two appealing, small-scale projects that can be built by beginners for immediate satisfaction.

Parson's tables are attractive in any size or variation. We built one as a cherry coffee table with a plywood-veneer top, and the other as a huge oak dining table with a top made of tongue-and-groove flooring. Except for the tops and some detailing on the legs, the basic structure is the same.

A beautiful mirror frame can be the finishing touch for any room in your house. If you've never mitered corners, you can get experience by building the first project in this chapter, the bookcase lamp.

No matter where you start, each project leads to another, the skills required in one pertain to those in another, and in time you could build them all!

BOOKCASE LAMP

So named not because it sits on a bookcase but because this lamp actually *is* a bookcase. It makes a perfect, unusual gift for a bibliophile, as several paperbacks will fit in its base. It is also a good project to start with if you've never done mitering.

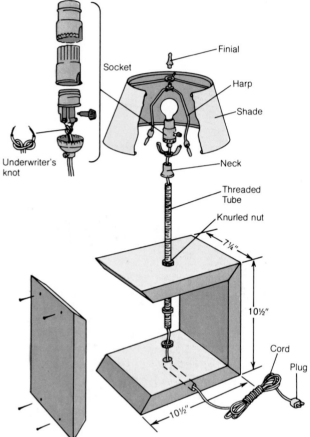

CONSTRUCTION

Step 1. Miter the corners of the wood at a 45-degree angle (see page 86).

Step 2. Drill a ⅜-inch hole in the center of the top and bottom.

Step 3. Drill a ⅜-inch hole through the back edge of the bottom so it meets the center hole, as shown.

Step 4. Glue and nail together the top, bottom, and sides. Set the nails (see page 96) and fill the holes.

Step 5. Secure the threaded tube to the top and bottom with the three knurled nuts, as shown.

Step 6. Thread the cord through the hole in the back and up through the tube.

Step 7. Attach the cord to the socket and assemble the rest of the lamp.

Step 8. Sand and finish the wood.

LUMBER TO BUY	MILL TO	FOR PROJECT PIECE
Redwood (grade A select)		
1 2″× 8″× 4′	4 1½″× 7¼″× 10½″	Lamp base

Hardware & Miscellaneous			
8d finishing nails		1	finial
1 ⅜″ dia.× 12″ brass threaded tube		1	lamp shade
3 flat knurled nuts to fit tube		1	6′ or 8′ lamp cord with plug
1 decorative neck			Wood putty
1 lamp harp			Glue
1 lamp socket			

GLOBE LAMP

Here's a chance to build something small, attractive, and inexpensive while getting in practice for some of the larger projects in this book. This globe lamp has two fairly intricate construction steps for the beginner, yet it's really easy to make. We chose oak, but use whatever you like.

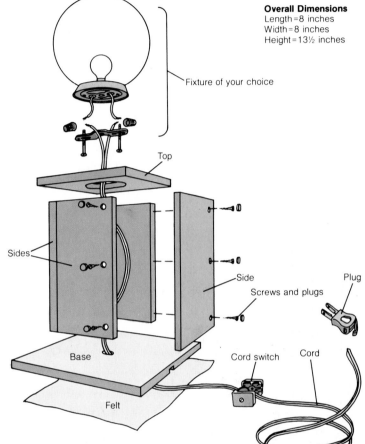

Overall Dimensions
Length = 8 inches
Width = 8 inches
Height = 13½ inches

Fixture of your choice

Top

Sides

Base

Side

Screws and plugs

Plug

Felt

Cord switch

Cord

CONSTRUCTION

Step 1. Mill all the pieces.

Step 2. Glue and screw the four sides together as shown. Countersink the screws with a ⅜-inch bit and drill a ³/₃₂-inch pilot hole for each screw in the center of the ⅜-inch holes (see page 00); then plug.

Step 3. Cut or drill whatever holes are needed in the top to accommodate the light fixture. Check the fit of the fixture, then remove it and set it aside.

Step 4. Drill a ⅜-inch hole in the center of the bottom. Rout a groove ¼-inch wide by ³/₁₆-inch deep in the middle of the piece from the drilled hole to one edge to make a path for the cord.

Step 5. When the glue is dry, then clean, sand, and finish the top, sides, and bottom.

Step 6. Attach the fixture and cord.

Step 7. Screw the top to the sides, then countersink and dowel-plug the screws.

Step 8. Thread the cord through the hole in the bottom and attach the bottom to the sides with four screws. Do not countersink or plug these screws.

Step 9. Lay the cord in the routed groove and glue the felt to the bottom.

Step 10. Attach the switch and plug.

LUMBER TO BUY		MILL TO		FOR PROJECT PIECE
Oak (FAS grade)				
1	2″ × 10″ × 8″	1	1¾″ × 8″ × 8″	Base
1	1″ × 8″ × 5′	1	¾″ × 7″ × 7″	Top
		4	¾″ × 5½″ × 12″	Sides
Dowel				
1	⅜″ dia. × 1′	12	⅜″ dia. × ½″	Dowel plugs

Hardware & Miscellaneous			
16	1½″ × #8 flat-head wood screws	1	cord switch
4	2½″ × #8 flat-head wood screws	1	plug
1	lamp fixture	1	felt piece 8″ × 8″
6′	lamp cord		Glue

SHOJI LIGHT

In keeping with the classic Japanese shoji design, this light is extremely adaptable and integrates attractively with many styles. It is simple to build, and can be used standing vertically or horizontally, or mounted on a wall or a ceiling. However you use it, you will have a beautiful sculpture and a lot of soft, warm light that is easy on the eyes.

CONSTRUCTION

Step 1. Mill all the pieces.

Step 2. Cut a ½-inch deep rabbet halfway through the plywood (⅜ inch) in the back edge of the top, bottom, and sides to accommodate the back (see page 87).

Step 3. Cut a ¾-inch deep rabbet halfway through the front edge of the top, bottom, and sides to accommodate the plastic sheet and the face strips.

Step 4. Glue and nail (with brads) the side top-edge strips to cover the end grain.

Step 5. Drill a ¼-inch hole in the center of the back about 1 inch from the bottom for the electric cord, and a ¾-inch finger-hole at the center of the back near the top so you can remove the panel easily when you need to replace the lights. Drill 10 pilot holes (one on each end and three on each side) for the #4 wood screws to insert the back in place.

Step 6. Mount the fluorescent fixtures to the back. They should be centered about 10 inches apart and equidistant from the sides.

Step 7. Wire the fixtures together and to the electric cord with the wire nuts. Thread the cord through the ¼-inch hole in the back.

Step 8. Glue and nail together the top, bottom, and sides.

Step 9. Set and screw the plywood back into its rabbet.

Step 10 (optional). Glue and nail the feet to the bottom of the case. If you plan to mount the light, attach the appropriate flush-mounting hardware to the back of the top.

Step 11. Stain, oil, or otherwise finish the case and all the remaining strips before proceeding.

Step 12. Lay the case on its back and set the plastic sheet into the front rabbet.

Step 13. Lay the face strips on top of the plastic. Drill a ¹⁄₁₆-inch pilot hole through the ends of each strip and the plastic, and drive a 6-penny nail through each hole to hold the strips and plastic in place.

Step 14. Nail the front edges to the top, bottom, and sides to cover the edge of the plastic and the ends of the face strips. A dab of glue where they cross will keep the lines square through changes in humidity and temperature.

Step 15. Attach the plug to the cord and mount the cord switch, and you're ready to position the light.

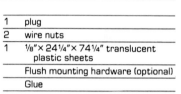

LUMBER TO BUY		MILL TO		FOR PROJECT PIECE
Cherry plywood				
1	¾″ × 4′ × 8′	2	¾″ × 9½″ × 75″	Sides
		2	¾″ × 9½″ × 25″	Top and bottom
Cherry (FAS grade)				
1	1″ × 3″ × 8′	2	⁵⁄₁₆″ × ¾″ × 75 ⁵⁄₁₆″	Side front edges
		2	⁵⁄₁₆″ × ¾″ × × 9½″	Side top edges
		2	⁵⁄₁₆″ × ¾″ × 25″	Top & bottom front edges
		2	⁵⁄₁₆″ × ¾″ × 74¼″	Vertical face strips
		7	⁵⁄₁₆″ × ¾″ × 24¼″	Horizontal face strips
1	2″ × 2″ × 2′	2	1¾″ × 1¾″ × 9″	Feet (optional)
Fir plywood (CD grade)				
1	½″ × 4′ × 8′	1	½″ × 24¼″ × 74¼″	Back

Hardware & Miscellaneous			
	¾″ brads	1	plug
10	¾″ × #4 wood screws	2	wire nuts
	6d finishing nails	1	⅛″ × 24¼″ × 74¼″ translucent plastic sheets
2	6′ one-tube fluorescent fixtures		Flush mounting hardware (optional)
8′	electric cord		Glue
1	cord switch		

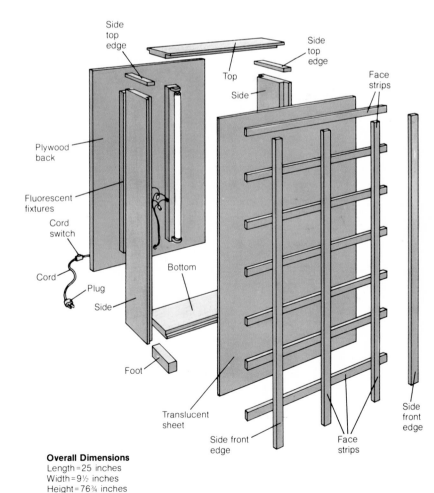

Overall Dimensions
Length = 25 inches
Width = 9½ inches
Height = 76¾ inches

MAGAZINE RACK

This rack may be just what you need to eliminate clutter, and its simplicity makes it a good beginning project for a novice woodworker. You will learn four basic skills, and can build this with or without power tools. The dowels are part of the design of this rack, not for categorizing your reading, and make the rack easy to build.

CONSTRUCTION

Step 1. Mill all the pieces.

Step 2. Put a mark 11½ inches from the end of each side. Cut lap joints the width of the pieces halfway through the wood (see page 87).

Step 3. Lay out the dowel-hole placement on the cross-pieces; mark the first 1⅛ inches from the end and continue the remaining marks 1¼ inches on center. Drill the holes slightly deeper than ¼ inch (see page 89).

Step 4. Sand all the pieces.

Step 5. Drill and counterbore holes in the sides for screws and ½-inch plugs (see page 89).

Step 6. Tap the dowels into the center cross-pieces, then set another cross-piece on top of the dowel ends and start inserting the dowels from one end to the other, making sure they are equally housed. Afterwards, tap the cross-piece to secure the dowels.

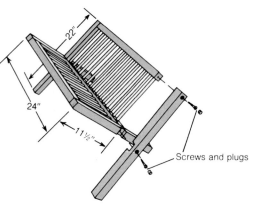

Screws and plugs

Step 7. Tap the second row of dowels into the center cross-piece and then add the third cross-piece.

Step 8. Glue and screw the sides to the ends of the cross-pieces.

Step 9. Glue and plug the counterbores with short pieces of scrap dowel, or cut ½-inch plugs from scrap redwood (see page 89). Cut and sand the plugs flush after the glue has dried.

Step 10. Finish as desired.

LUMBER TO BUY	MILL TO		FOR PROJECT PIECE
Redwood (grade A select)			
2 2″× 2″× 6′	4	1½″× 1½″× 22″	Sides
	3	1½″× 1½″× 21″	Cross-pieces
Dowel			
8 ½″ dia.× 4′	32	½″ dia.× 10½″	Supports

Hardware & Miscellaneous
6 2½″× #10 flat-head wood screws
Glue

FIREWOOD TOWER

Firewood becomes an ever-changing sculpture in this tower, which takes up barely over a square foot of floor space and holds three or four times the firewood of a conventional box. We used mahogany for durability, and a stain and wax finish. This is one of the easiest projects in this book, and requires very few tools.

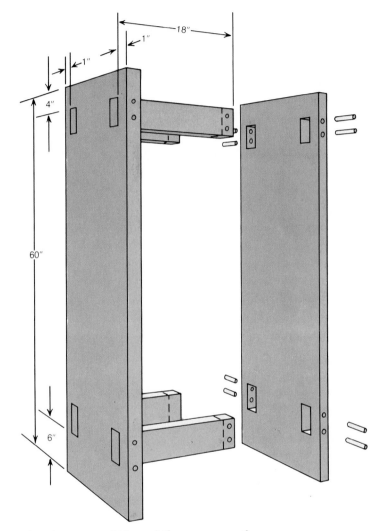

CONSTRUCTION

Step 1. Mill all the lumber.

Step 2. Mark the position of the mortises on the tower sides (see illustration for placement), and trace their outlines around the end of a cross-piece.

Step 3. Drill a starting hole for each mortise and then cut it out with a saber or key-hole saw; or drill out the majority of the material and chisel out the mortise to square. Cut on the inside of the outline to avoid making the mortise too small; you can always enlarge it with a rasp.

Step 4. Insert the cross-pieces into the mortises, drill the holes for the dowel

pins (see page 89), and then remove the cross-pieces.

Step 5. Put glue in each mortise and insert the cross-pieces again.

Step 6. Glue the dowels, drive them home with a rubber mallet, and let the glue dry. Then use a hand saw to cut them flush with the surface.

Step 7. Clean and sand all the surfaces and finish as desired.

LUMBER TO BUY		MILL TO		FOR PROJECT PIECE
(Mahogany (FAS grade)				
2	2″× 12″× 5′	2	1¾″× 11½″× 5′	Sides
1	2″× 4″× 6′	4	1¾″× 3½″× 18″	Cross-pieces
Dowel				
1	½″ dia.× 4′	16	½″ dia.× 3″	Pins

DISPLAY BOXES

Use these as individual boxes, stack them on a shelf, screw them to a wall, or glue them together to make a freestanding unit. However you join them, the pieces must be milled accurately and the joints perfectly square. The 16 boxes illustrated can be made from our list of supplies: four 9 by 9, six 6 by 6, three 12 by 12, and three 6 by 12 inches.

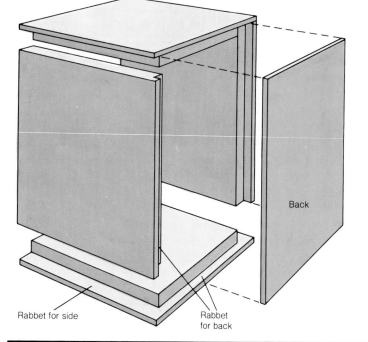

Same construction for several sizes of box

Back

Rabbet for side

Rabbet for back

CONSTRUCTION

Step 1. Mill all the pieces.

Step 2. For the side joints, cut a rabbet on both ends of all the 6-inch, 12-inch, and 9-inch pieces to ⅛ inch of the side and exactly the width of the boards (see page 87).

Step 3. Cut a rabbet on the inside back edge of all the boards to accept the plywood backs. The rabbets should be cut just a bit deeper than ⅛ inch and to within ¼ inch of the outside edge of the boards.

Step 4. Glue and clamp or glue and nail the boxes together.

Step 5. Glue and nail the backs onto the boxes.

Step 6. When the glue is dry, clean and finish the boxes.

LUMBER	MILL TO	FOR PROJECT PIECE
Walnut (FAS grade)		
48 1″×6″ boards	12 pieces × 6″	Sides
	18 pieces × 5¾″	Tops and bottoms
	12 pieces × 12″	Sides
	6 pieces × 11¾″	Tops and bottoms
	8 pieces × 9″	Sides
	8 pieces × 8¾″	Tops and bottoms
Walnut plywood		
1 ⅛″×48″×48″	6 5⅝″×5⅜″	Backs
	3 5⅝″×11⅜″	
	3 11⅝″×11⅜″	
	4 8⅝″×8⅜″	

Hardware & Miscellaneous
½″ brads (optional)
Glue

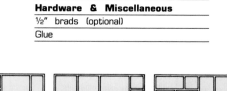

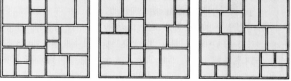

Three of the many ways these boxes can be assembled into a rectangle

FOLDING SCREEN

Here is a practical, attractive way to divide or accent an area without using much floor space. You can use the three-panel screen as it is, or add fabric to enrich its possibilities. You can change the width of the panels without changing the height; the proportions will hold. And, of course, you can use any wood.

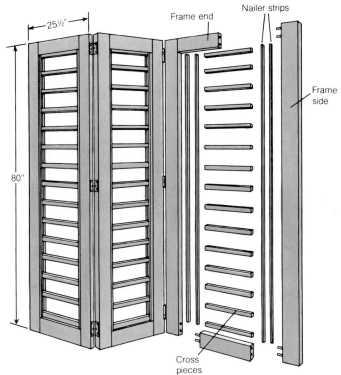

CONSTRUCTION

Step 1. Mill all the lumber.

Step 2. Glue and dowel the frame ends between the frame sides (see page 89).

Step 3. Attach nailer strips to one side of each frame with finishing nails.

Step 4. Turn the frames over and place the cross-pieces on 4⅜-inch centers against the nailer strip. Toe-nail them to the frame with a nail in each end. (If you plan to weave fabric through the cross-pieces, set aside the top and bottom pieces.)

Step 5. Nail the remaining nailer strips to the frame on top of the cross-pieces.

Step 6. Sand and finish the screen before assembling.

Step 7 (optional). Cut each fabric insert 80 inches long and 22 inches wide (more if you plan to hem the sides). If you weave the fabric through the cross-pieces—a variation not shown in the photo—the ends can be sewn to hold the cross-pieces, or folded over and nailed to them. Insert the bottom cross-piece and fabric between the nailer strips, and nail the cross-piece in place. Weave the fabric over and under the cross-pieces until you reach the top. Insert the top cross-piece into the hem, or fold and nail the fabric to it and nail it in place between the strips. You can also tack or staple the fabric to the back of each panel.

Step 8. Hinge the joint of each panel on a different side so the screen folds like an accordion. For a more professional job, inset the hinges by tracing their outlines on the sides of each panel with a pencil or sharp knife, and chisel away the wood to the thickness of the hinge. Then mount.

LUMBER TO BUY			MILL TO		FOR PROJECT PIECE
Cherry (FAS grade)					
6	2″× 3″× 7′		6	1¾″× 2½″× 80″	Frame sides
2	2″× 3″× 6′		6	1¾″× 2½″× 22″	Frame ends
15	1″× 1″× 6′		45	⅞″× ⅞″× 22″	Cross-pieces
3	1″× 1″× 7′		12	⅜″× ⅜″× 75″	Nailer strips

Hardware & Miscellaneous	
3d finishing nails	⅜″ grooved dowels (24)
1″ brads	Fabric (optional): 8 yds. of 36″ fabric or 5 yds. of 45″ fabric
3 pair 3″ brass loose-pin butt hinges	Glue

MIRROR FRAME

Here's a perfect finishing touch—a framed wall mirror that will add tremendously to any room the instant it's hung. You can copy our model exactly, if you wish, or have fun playing with different woods and shapes. Our choice of wood was mahogany, accented with narrow strips of maple.

LUMBER TO BUY		MILL TO		FOR PROJECT PIECE
Mahogany (FAS grade)				
2	1″× 4″× 8′	2	³⁄₄″× 3¹⁄₂″× 8′	A
		2	³⁄₄″× 2¹⁄₂″× 8′	B
		16	³⁄₄″× 2¹⁄₈″× 8′	D
		2	³⁄₈″× 1″× 8′	E
		2	³⁄₄″× 1″× 8′	G
Maple (FAS grade)				
2	1″× 3″× 8′	2	¹⁄₄″× 2″× 8′	C
		2	¹⁄₄″× 1″× 8′	F
Fir plywood				
1	¹⁄₄″× 2′× 8′	1	¹⁄₄″× 50¹⁄₂″× 32¹⁄₂″	Back
Maple or birch dowel				
1	¹⁄₂″ dia.× 1′	8	¹⁄₂″ dia.× ¹⁄₂″	Dowel plugs

Hardware & Miscellaneous

3d finishing nails

8 2¹⁄₂″× #10 flat-head wood screws

16 ⁵⁄₈″× #4 flat-head wood screws

1 plate glass mirror (ordered to fit the finished frame)

Sturdy, flush wall-mounting hardware

Glue

CONSTRUCTION

Step 1. Rip the lumber into the strips indicated, or decide what the cross-section of your molding will look like and mill the stock accordingly.

Step 2. Rout the edges of the shaped pieces. We made two passes with a router on the G piece: the first with a ½-inch cove bit, and the second with a ½-inch-radius round-over bit.

Step 3. Rabbet the bottom piece (B) for the mirror and the plywood back. The first cut, for the mirror, is ½-inch deep by ⅜ inch; the second, for the plywood, is ¼-inch deep by ⅝ inch.

Step 4. Glue and nail or clamp the strips together as shown in the cross-section, in the order of their letters. If you use finishing nails, mark the general areas where cuts will be made so you don't put nails there, and place them a foot or two apart to hold the strips until the glue sets. (It helps to drill 1/32-inch pilot holes through the first piece the nail must penetrate.)

Step 5. When the glue is dry, cut the molding into four pieces, mitering both ends of each piece 45 degrees. Our frame was made of two pieces 37 inches long, and two pieces 55 inches long.

Step 6. Mark the ends of the pieces so they don't get mixed up, then check each corner in turn and adjust the fit with a block plane.

Step 7. To assemble the frame, clamp the pieces to your workbench, then drill two pilot holes and counterbores for screws and dowel plugs in the sides at each corner (see page 89). Glue the mitered surfaces and insert the #10 screws.

Step 8. Glue the ½-inch dowel plugs into the counterbores. When the glue has set, cut and sand them flush with the surface.

Step 9. Clean, sand, and finish the frame.

Step 10. With the frame face down, lay the mirror in its rabbet, then insert the plywood back on top of the mirror and secure it with the #4 screws.

Step 11. Affix sturdy, flush wall-mounting hardware to the back of the frame to hang it securely.

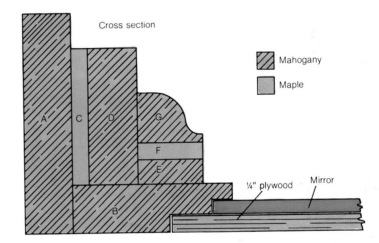

Cross section

Mahogany

Maple

A C D G F E B

¼" plywood Mirror

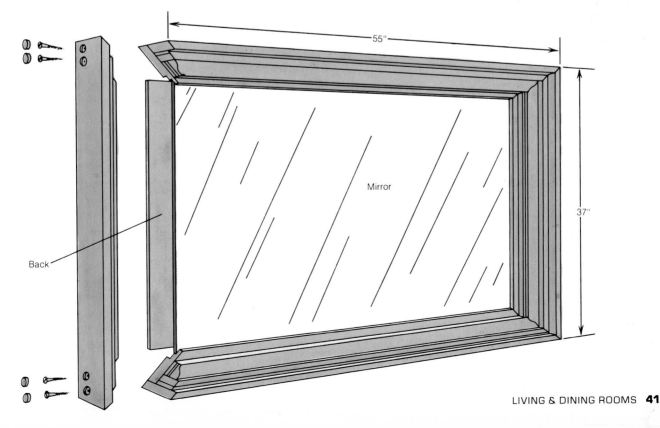

55"

37"

Mirror

Back

GLASS-TOP TABLES

Add beautiful material to classic lines, and the whole becomes greater than the sum of its parts. Moreover, these tables are astonishingly easy to build. The heights we've given are standard; the widths and lengths can be varied. For a cocktail table, the skirts would be the size you want less 5 inches (the width of two legs); for a larger table, deduct 6 inches for the legs. The glass is 1⅝ inches less than the table dimensions.

CONSTRUCTION

Step 1. Mill all the pieces.

Step 2. Mark and drill dowel holes where the skirts join the legs (see page 89), then glue and clamp all the pieces together.

Step 3. Mark a square on the inside of each leg, leaving ¾ inch on two sides (see illustration). Using the outside skirts as the base surface for a router, cut away the squares ¼-inch deep. This will allow the glass to sit flush with the continuous skirt edging. The router leaves a rounded corner, which then must be chiseled square while smoothing the end-grain surface just cut by the router.

Step 4. Sand and finish as desired.

Step 5. Set the glass in place.

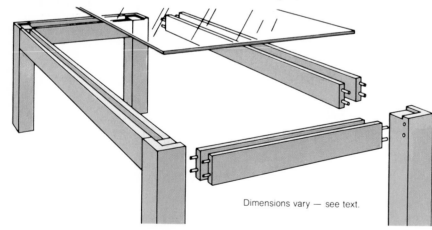

Dimensions vary — see text.

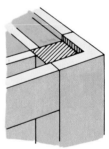

Rout shaded area
¼ inch deep for glass.

Cocktail table (20"× 34")

LUMBER TO BUY	MILL TO	FOR PROJECT PIECE
Walnut (FAS grade)		
1 3"× 3"× 6'	4 2½"× 2½"× 17"	Legs
3 1"× 4"× 6'	4 ¾"× 3½"× 31"	Skirt sides
	4 ¾"× 3½"× 15"	Skirt ends

Hardware & Miscellaneous
1 ¼"× 18⅜"× 32⅜" glass plate
32 ⅜"× 2" grooved dowels
Glue

Sofa Table (14"× 66")

LUMBER TO BUY	MILL TO	FOR PROJECT PIECE
Walnut (FAS grade)		
1 4"× 4"× 6'	4 3"× 3"× 34"	Legs
4 1"× 4"× 6'	4 ¾"× 3½"× 60"	Skirt sides
	4 ¾"× 3½"× 8"	Skirt ends

Hardware & Miscellaneous
1 ¼"× 12⅜"× 64⅜" glass plate
32 ⅜"× 2" grooved dowels
Glue

COFFEE TABLE

The uncluttered lines of parson's tables makes them compatible with all styles of furnishings, and the pattern can be adapted to various sizes—as you'll see by turning the page. These tables are easy to build, and are enriched by your choice of wood. This coffee table has a pretty detail where the cherry plywood butts to the skirt.

CONSTRUCTION

Step 1. Mill all the pieces.

Step 2. Cut notches ¾ inch by 3½ inches in two sides of each leg-top to accept the rails.

Step 3. Glue and screw the rails to the legs, staggering the #12 screws so they don't interfere with each other. Countersink and conceal them with ½-inch dowel plugs (see page 89).

Step 4. Glue and screw the braces ¾-inch below the top of the rails as shown. Countersink and plug the #12 screws in the 22-inch braces as you did the legs, and use the #10 screws to attach the other braces to the rails from the inside.

Step 5. Glue the plywood in place and screw it through the braces from the bottom. (One screw in each brace is sufficient.)

Step 6. Sand the top carefully and evenly to avoid going through the veneer, and be careful not to put cross-grain scratches on the end rails. Finish as desired.

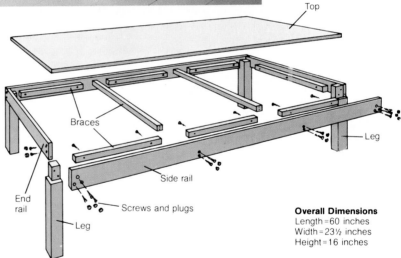

Overall Dimensions
Length = 60 inches
Width = 23½ inches
Height = 16 inches

LUMBER TO BUY		MILL TO		FOR PROJECT PIECE
Cherry (FAS grade)				
1	4"× 4"× 6'	4	3½"× 3½"× 14¼"	Legs
2	1"× 4"× 8'	2	¾"× 3½"× 60"	Side rails
		2	¾"× 3½"× 22"	End rails
Poplar or alder (FAS grade)				
2	2"× 2"× 6'	2	1¼"× 1¼"× 22"	Braces
		6	1¼"× 1¼"× 16"	
		2	1¼"× 1¼"× 14"	
Cherry plywood				
1	¾"× 2'× 5'	1	¾"× 22"× 58½"	Top
Dowel				
1	½" dia.× 1'	20	½" dia.× ½"	Dowel plugs

Hardware & Miscellaneous
20 2"× #12 flat-head wood screws
42 1¾"× #10 flat-head wood screws
Glue

OAK PARSON'S TABLE

This table will accommodate 10 easily for a capital feast—if your dining room will support it. If not, change the dimensions; parson's tables are attractive at any size. The flooring-strip top makes this one unusual, and surprisingly easy to build. You can use any hardwood that comes in flooring strips, and less expensive or scrap hardwood for the invisible bracing.

LUMBER TO BUY	MILL TO		FOR PROJECT PIECE
Oak (FAS grade)			
6 2″× 6″× 6′	12	1½″× 4½″× 27½″	Legs
2 2″× 5″× 10′	2	1½″× 4″× 82″	Side rails
1 2″× 5″× 8′	2	1½″× 4″× 38″	End rails
Poplar or alder			
5 2″× 2″× 5′	2	1¾″× 1¾″× 38″	Braces
	4	1¾″× 1¾″× 29″	
	1	1¾″× 1¾″× 20″	
Oak T&G flooring strips			
16 ¾″× 2½″× 7′	16	¾″× 2½″× 79″	Top
Plywood (CD grade)			
1 ¾″× 4′× 8′	1	¾″× 38″× 79″	Insert

Hardware & Miscellaneous
20 3½″× #12 flat-head wood screws
24 3″× #12 flat-head wood screws
6d finishing nails
3d finishing nails
½″ dia. doweling
Glue

CONSTRUCTION

Step 1. Mill all the pieces.

Step 2. Glue and clamp the leg pieces to form the 4½-inch by 4½-inch legs.

Step 3. When the glue is dry, notch two sides of the top of each leg to accept the rails (see illustration). The notches should measure 1¾ by 4 inches.

Step 4. Glue and attach the rails to the legs with the 3½-inch screws, staggering the screws so they don't interfere with each other. Countersink and conceal the screws with ½-inch doweling or plugs cut to match (see page 89).

Step 5. Position the braces 1½ inches below the top of the rails and glue and screw them to the rails as shown, using the 3½-inch screws. Countersink and plug the 38-inch braces. Use the 3-inch screws to attach the other braces to the rails from the inside.

Step 6. Glue and nail the plywood insert to the bracing with 6-penny finishing nails.

Step 7. The oak flooring is laid on top of the plywood, a strip at a time, running flush with the rails. Each strip will be toe-nailed in place; nailing may be easier if you drill ⅟₁₆-inch pilot holes into the strips at the proper angle. Apply glue to the back of the first strip, knock it tight against the rail, and toe-nail it to the plywood with 3-penny nails. Lay the second and succeeding strips in the same manner, knocking each tight against the preceding one until the top is complete. The last strip will have to be ripped to fit.

Step 8. Sand and finish as desired.

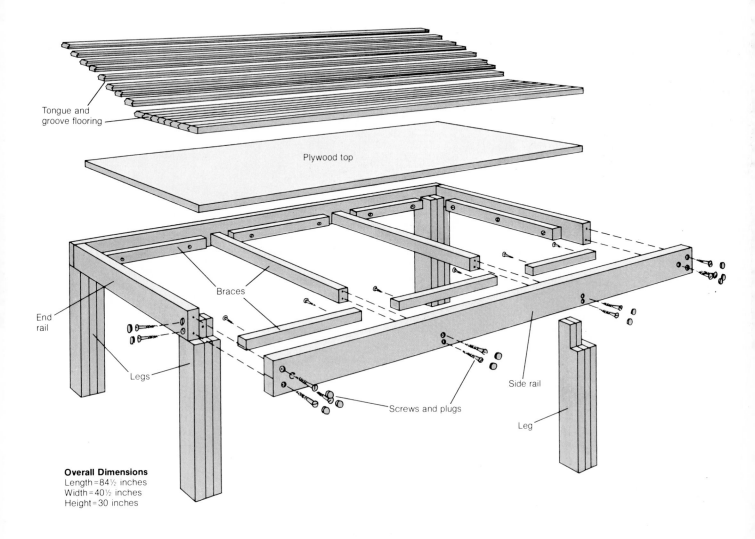

Tongue and groove flooring

Plywood top

Braces

End rail

Legs

Screws and plugs

Side rail

Leg

Overall Dimensions
Length = 84½ inches
Width = 40½ inches
Height = 30 inches

MODULAR UNITS

These four basic pieces are incredibly flexible and each is easy to build.
Their proportions are excellent, so the scale will hold whatever you do
with them. The chests can be used singly, as end tables; stacked three-
or four-high to make a beautiful dresser; placed side-by-side as buffets;
combined with sandwich drawers and high or low pedestals to make a
commodious desk (shown on page 59); or used to house records and
stereo equipment.

We've provided seven variations of the chest, and two pedestal sizes.
The drawer sandwich combines with the chests in multiple ways, and
the adjustable shelves are for books or display. Use the units as room
dividers, too: the backs are as nice as the fronts.

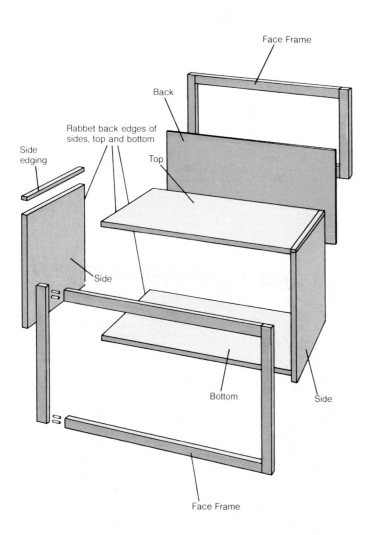

Face Frame

Back

Rabbet back edges of
sides, top and bottom

Side
edging

Top

Side

Side

Bottom

Face Frame

Overall Dimensions
Length = 18 inches
Width = 30 inches
Height = 20 inches

BASIC CHEST CONSTRUCTION

Step 1. Mill all the pieces.

Step 2. Cut rabbets ¼-inch deep in the top, bottom, and sides to accept the ¼-inch plywood back (see page 87). Also drill holes for the adjustable-shelf clips and rabbet grooves for partitions if applicable.

Step 3. Glue and clamp or nail the edging to the side tops.

Step 4. Assemble the face frames with glue and dowels (see page 89).

Step 5. Assemble the top, bottom, and sides with glue and clamps or nails. If your chest has a dust panel or partitions, assemble those too.

Step 6. Tack the back in place with the best side facing out, so you can use the unit as a room divider.

Step 7. Glue and clamp or nail the face frames to both sides.

Step 8. Follow the instructions on page 92 to build the drawers, and the illustrations and materials lists to build the doors. Note that all dimensions are for flush-inset doors and drawers. For other styles and directions for adjusting measurements, see pages 24 and 91.

Step 9. Install the doors and drawers (see page 92).

Step 10. Set the nails and fill the holes (see page 96), then sand and finish as desired. (Sand the veneer lightly and carefully so as not to go through it, and avoid putting cross-grain scratches in the cherry frames.)

Step 11. Install pulls, catches, and shelf as needed.

MATERIALS FOR ONE BASIC CHEST			
LUMBER TO BUY		**MILL TO**	**FOR PROJECT PIECE**
Cherry plywood			
1	¾" × 4' × 8'	2	¾" × 16½" × 19¾"	Sides
		2	¾" × 16½" × 28½"	Top and bottom
		1	¾" × 16" × 28¼"	Adjustable shelf
1	¼" × 2' × 3'	1	¼" × 18½" × 29¼"	Back
Cherry (FAS grade)			
1	1" × 2" × 7'	4	¾" × 1½" × 20"	Face frame verticals
1	1" × 2" × 10'	4	¾" × 1½" × 27"	Face frame horizontals
Scrap cherry			
		2	¼" × ¾" × 16½"	Side edging
		1	¼" × ¾" × 28¼"	Shelf edging

Hardware & Miscellaneous	
6d finishing nails	Door and drawer pulls
4d finishing nails	Door catches
Wood putty	Shelf clips
Glue	Hinges

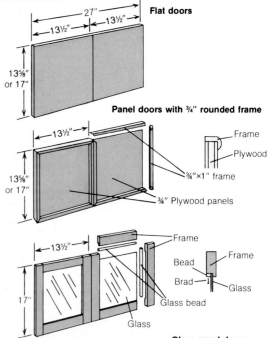

Flat doors

27"

13½"   13½"

13⅝"
or 17"

Panel doors with ¾" rounded frame

13½"

Frame

Plywood

¾" × 1" frame

13⅝"
or 17"

¾" Plywood panels

13½"

Frame

Bead

Brad

Frame

Glass

Glass bead

Glass

17"

Glass panel doors

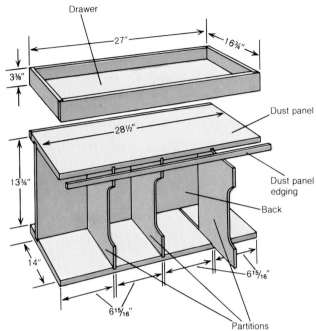

Drawer

27" 16¾"

3⅜"

28½" Dust panel

13¾" Dust panel edging

Back

14"

6¹⁵⁄₁₆"

6¹⁵⁄₁₆"

Partitions

CHEST VARIATIONS

LUMBER TO BUY	MILL TO		FOR PROJECT PIECE
Flat doors (1 pair)			
Cherry plywood			
¾"× 1½'× 2½'	1	17"× 27" (cut in half)	Doors
Panel doors with rounded frame (1 pair)			
Cherry plywood			
¾"× 1½'× 2½'	2	16½"× 13"	Panels
Cherry (FAS grade)			
2 1"× 2"× 6'	4	1"× 17"	Frames
	4	1"× 13½"	
Glass panel doors, 2" flat frame (1 pair)			
Cherry (FAS grade)			
2 1"× 3"× 6'	4	2"× 17"	Frames
	4	2"× 10"	
Cherry scraps	4	¼"× ⅜"× 10"	Glass beads
	4	¼"× ⅜"× 13"	
Glass			
(⅛" single strength)	2	13½"× 10"	Panels
Flat doors below drawer (1 pair)			
Cherry plywood			
¾"× 1½'× 2½'	1	13⅝"× 27" (cut in half)	Doors
Panel doors below drawer, with rounded frame			
Cherry plywood			
¾"× 1½'× 2½'	2	12⅝"× 12⅝"	Panels
Cherry (FAS grade)			
2 1"× 2"× 6'	8	1"× 13½"	Frames
Dust panel below drawer			
Cherry plywood			
¾"× 1½'× 2½'	1	16"× 28½"	Panel
Cherry scrap			
	1	¼"× ¾"× 28½"	Edging
Partitions for record storage			
Cherry plywood			
¼"× 3'× 4'	1	14"× 28½"	Back
	3	14"× 13"	Dividers (with cut-out front edge; see drawing)
Drawer			
Cherry (FAS grade)			
1 1"× 4"× 3'	1	3⅜"× 27"	Front
½" mahogany			
(drawer stock)	2	3⅜"× 16½"	Sides
	1	2⅞"× 25¹⁵⁄₁₆"	Back
Mahogany (or other inexpensive) plywood			
¼"× 1½'× 2½'	1	16⅜"× 26⅜"	Bottom

PEDESTAL CONSTRUCTION

Step 1. Mill all the pieces and miter the corners (see page 86). Or, you can reduce the length of the sides by 1½ inches and of the front and back by ½-inch, then glue pieces of ¼-inch by ¾-inch edging over the end grain on the front and back.

Step 2. Assemble the pedestals with glue and nails. Set the nails and fill the holes.

Step 3. Sand and finish as desired.

MATERIALS FOR PEDESTALS

LUMBER TO BUY	MILL TO		FOR PROJECT PIECE
Cherry plywood			
1 ¾"× 2'× 3'	2	3¼"× 28¼"	Front and back
	2	3¼"× 16¼"	Sides
	4	3¼"× 3¼" triangles	Corner blocks
High Pedestal			
Cherry plywood			
1 ¾"× 3'× 4'	2	6½"× 28¼"	Front and back
	2	6½"× 16¼"	Sides
	2	3¼"× 3¼" triangles	Corner blocks

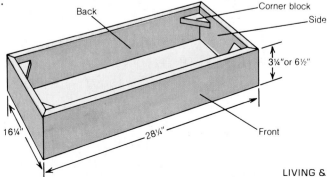

Back Corner block

Side

3¼"or 6½"

16¼"

28¼" Front

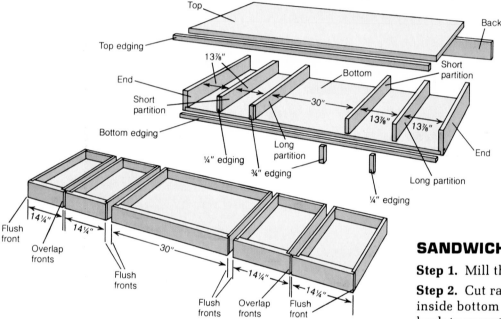

Top

Top edging

Back

13⅞″

End

Bottom

Short partition

Short partition

30″

Bottom edging

13⅞″

13⅞″

¼″ edging

Long partition

¾″ edging

End

Long partition

¼″ edging

Overall Dimensions
Length=90 inches
Width=18 inches
Height=4¼ inches

14¼″

Flush front

14¼″

Overlap fronts

30″

Flush fronts

14¼″

Flush fronts

14¼″

Overlap fronts

Flush front

SANDWICH CONSTRUCTION

Step 1. Mill the case pieces.

Step 2. Cut rabbets ⅜-inch deep in the inside bottom edge of the sides and back to accept the ½-inch plywood bottom.

Step 3. Glue and clamp or nail the edging to the top, bottom, and partitions as shown. The thicker edging is for the 17-inch partitions and extends ½ inch below the bottom edge.

Step 4. Assemble all the pieces with glue and clamps or nails. Make sure the joints are square and the dimensions between the partitions are accurate.

Step 5. Mill the drawer pieces.

Step 6. Assemble the drawers after dadoing grooves for the drawer bottoms and rabbeting the drawer fronts (see page 91). Four of the drawers must be made to overlap the partitions, so the appropriate rabbets should be ⅞-inch deep. (See illustration.)

Step 7. Set the visible nails, fill the holes, then sand and finish as desired.

Step 8. Install drawer pulls.

MATERIALS FOR SANDWICH DRAWERS

LUMBER TO BUY		MILL TO	FOR PROJECT PIECE
Cherry plywood			
1 ¾″× 2′× 8′	1	¾″× 16½″× 88″	Top
	2	¾″× 3″× 17″	Partitions
	2	¾″× 3″× 16¼″	
Mahogany (or other inexpensive) plywood			
1 ½″× 2′× 8′	1	½″× 17⅜″× 89¼″	Bottom
Cherry (FAS grade)			
3 1″× 6″× 8′	2	¾″× 4¼″× 18″	Ends
	2	¾″× 4¼″× 88½″	Back
	1	¾″× ¾″× 88½″	Top edging
	2	¼″× ¾″× 3″	Partition edging
	2	¾″× ¾″× 3½″	
	1	¼″× ½″× 89¼″	Bottom edging
	1	¾″× 3⅜″× 30″	Drawer fronts
	4	¾″× 3⅜″× 14¼″	
½″ mahogany			
(drawer stock)	10	½″× 2¹⁵⁄₁₆″× 16¾″	Drawer sides
	1	½″× 2¹⁵⁄₁₆″× 28¹⁵⁄₁₆″	Drawer backs
	4	¼″× 2¹⁵⁄₁₆″× 12¹³⁄₁₆″	
Mahogany (or other inexpensive) plywood			
1 ¼″× 4′× 4′	1	¼″× 16⅝″× 29⅜″	Drawer bottoms
	4	¼″× 16⅝″× 13¼″	

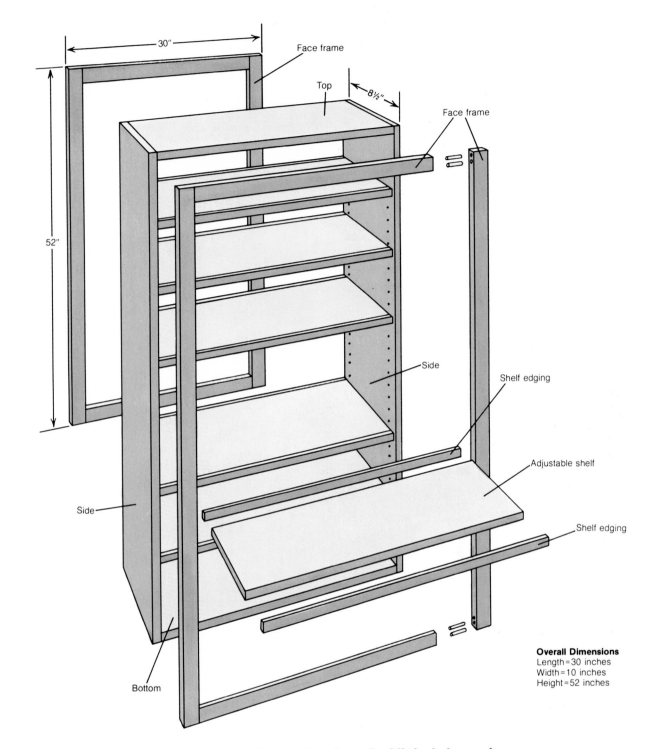

Overall Dimensions
Length = 30 inches
Width = 10 inches
Height = 52 inches

BOOK/DISPLAY CASE CONSTRUCTION

Step 1. Mill all the pieces.

Step 2. Assemble the face frames with glue and dowels (see page 89).

Step 3. Drill holes in the sides for the adjustable-shelf clips.

Step 4. Assemble the top, bottom, and sides with glue and clamps or nails.

Step 5. Glue and clamp or nail the face frames and edging to both sides of the case.

Step 6. Set the nails, fill the holes, and sand and finish as desired.

Step 7. Install the shelves.

MATERIALS FOR BOOK/DISPLAY CASE

LUMBER TO BUY	MILL TO		FOR PROJECT PIECE
Cherry Plywood			
1 ¾″× 4′× 8′	2	¾″× 8½″× 28½″	Top and bottom
	2	¾″× 8½″× 52″	Sides
	6	¾″× 7⅞″× 28¼″	Adjustable shelves
Cherry (FAS grade)			
4 1″× 2″× 8′	4	¾″× 1½″× 52″	Face frames
	4	¾″× 1½″× 27″	
1 1″× 4″× 8′	12	¼″× ¾″× 28¼″	Shelf edging

• DESKS & STORAGE •

Some of the finer accents in any home are beautifully designed desks and storage units. Here are plans for two small wall desks, a desk that fits neatly into a corner, and one that lies easily atop a pair of filing cabinets, as well as plans for a children's storage unit, bathroom storage and a cellar wine rack.

There's a desk for almost any purpose and for everyone in the family; two small wall desks for telephone messages and household accounts; a special children's desk that can grow with its user; a space-saving corner desk and two large desks for home or office.

One of these is a filing-cabinet desk with an accompanying cubbyhole unit, and the other a magnificent spacious sandwich desk fit for an executive—assembled from parts of the modular units found in the last chapter.

We've designed special storage units for sports equipment and clothing, for bathrooms, and for wine connoisseurs; a large cedar chest that will repel insects if you leave the inside unfinished; and a children's center that will hold just about everything. The sports storage unit is easiest to build: a bit of skill with a saw and some gluing and nailing, and you'll soon have a unique roomy sports closet ready for painting.

The filing cabinet desk requires sawing only for the edging on a hollow-core door. If you've never worked with plastic laminate, this is a good place to start, since you'll simply need a rectangular piece for the top. The accompanying cubbyhole case makes desk-top storage easy and elegant.

One of the small desks fits around a wall telephone and has a bulletin board for messages, pockets for pads of paper and pencils, and space to hold phone books. The small hanging desk has a door that drops open for use, and the shelves inside make it particularly handy.

The corner desk is a great spacesaver, and has a plastic laminate top, which gives it a good writing surface. It can go in any corner in any room.

A desk, sitting bench, and optional work table are part of the children's center, and the bench and table fit under the desk, between a closed storage cabinet and open shelves for display. This is a spacious yet compact unit that will grow with a child, as the desk can be raised again and again.

Another easy project is the bathroom storage unit, which will make your bathroom look bigger. If it's too large for your bathroom, just make it smaller. Or change the knobs, use wood backing and shelves, and put it in any other room.

The cellar wine rack has lots of semicircles to saw, and may be a good project to build for a winemaker friend, perhaps in exchange for a supply of the product!

The cedar chest is definitely one to put your name in, for it will be handed down lovingly from generation to generation. Three large semicircles are needed for the lid supports, and beveled sawing for the lid slats. You can countersink and plug all the screws, or use brass screws and allow them to show. However you build this, the result will be glorious.

WALL-PHONE DESK

Here's the ideal project for writing notes near your wall phone, and for storing pencils, pads of paper, and the phone book. You'll learn a lot about rabbets building this desk, so it's a good one to prepare you for larger projects.

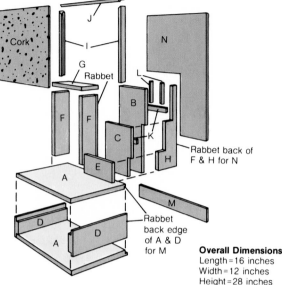

Overall Dimensions
Length = 16 inches
Width = 12 inches
Height = 28 inches

CONSTRUCTION

Step 1. Mill all the redwood.

Step 2. Cut a rabbet in the desk sides (D) where they will join the top and the bottom (see page 87).

Step 3. Cut a rabbet in the back edge of the desk pieces (A, D), the bulletin-board frame pieces (I, J), and one side of the telephone frame (F) and the slot side-piece (H) to accept the plywood back.

Step 4. Notch the slot side (H), the pencil-slot front (B), and the larger of the pad-slot fronts (C) so they fit together as shown.

Step 5. Nail the pencil and pad-slot bottoms (K) 3¼ inches from the top to the pencil-slot front (B) and to the larger

pad-slot front (C). Nail the pencil-slot dividers (L) to the pencil-slot front (B).

Step 6. Sand the pieces and assemble as follows, using glue and nails.

Step 7. Attach the three slot fronts (B, C, E) to the slot side (H).

Step 8. Attach the rabbeted phone-frame side (F) to the slot fronts (B, C, E).

Step 9. Assemble the rest of frame (F, G).

Step 10. Attach the phone frame and slot assembly to the desk top (A).

Step 11. Attach the desk sides (D) to the top and bottom (A).

Step 12. Nail the smaller piece of plywood (M) into the rabbeted desk back.

Step 13. Measure and cut the larger plywood back (N) to fit around the phone frame. Nail it on.

Step 14. Assemble the bulletin board frame (I, J). Attach to plywood back (N).

Step 15. Trim the cork exactly to fit the bulletin board area, spread glue on the plywood back, and smooth the cork into place.

Step 16. Clean, sand, and finish as you wish after the glue has dried.

LUMBER TO BUY		MILL TO		PROJECT PIECE	
Redwood (grade AB select)					
1	1"× 12"× 4'	2	¾"× 11¼"× 16"	Desk top/bottom	(A)
		1	¾"× 11¼"× 6½"	Pencil-slot front	(B)
		1	¾"× 6½"× 8"	Pad-slot front	(C)
1	1"× 4"× 8'	2	¾"× 3½"× 11½"	Desk sides	(D)
		1	¾"× 3½"× 7¼"	Pad-slot front	(E)
		2	¾"× 3½"× 12"	Phone-frame sides	(F)
		1	¾"× 3½"× 9½"	Phone-frame top	(G)
		1	¾"× 3½"× 12¾"	Slot side	(H)
1	1"× 2"× 6'	2	¾"× 1½"× 12"	Bulletin-board frame	(I)
		1	¾"× 1½"× 16"	Bulletin-board frame	(J)
		2	¾"× 1½"× 5¾"	Slot bottoms	(K)
		2	¾"× ⅜"× 3¼"	Pencil-slot dividers	(L)
Fir plywood (grade AD)					
1	¼"× 48"× 18"	1	¼"× 15¾"× 3"	Back	(M)
		1	¼"× 15½"× 24¾"	Back	(N)

Hardware & Miscellaneous
¼"× 12"× 16" cork
3d finishing nails
Glue

HANGING DESK

Here is a neat little disappearing desk for taking telephone messages or working on household accounts. We used birch because it has a good natural look if you want to leave it that way, and paints very well if you don't. A contrasting handle can give a nice finishing touch.

CONSTRUCTION

Step 1. Mill all the pieces.

Step 2. Dado grooves ½-inch deep for the partitions in the top and in the shelf (see page 87).

Step 3. Rabbet the top, bottom, and sides to accept the ¼-inch plywood back (see page 87).

Step 4. Glue and nail the top onto the sides, turn them over and attach the bottom in the same way, and glue and nail the shelf in place 4 inches from the top. Use a framing square to assure accuracy.

Step 5. Nail the back in place.

Step 6. Miter the two corners of the lip (see page 86), and glue and nail the lip 1 inch from the front and side edges with brads.

Step 7. Cut a rabbet ¼-inch deep by ¾-inch wide on the door edging.

Step 8. Round out the underside of the handle to fit the door and round over the top with a router, as shown.

Step 9. Glue and nail the edging and the handle to the door.

Step 10. Clean, sand, and finish the case, the partitions, and the door. (If you will be painting the desk, either use masking tape to protect the handle, or attach the handle after painting. In that case, don't paint the glue surface.)

Step 11. When the finish is dry, insert the partitions, hinge the door, and mount the lid supports and magnetic catches.

Note: If you plan to use a clear finish rather than paint, and don't want the joints to show where the sides connect to the top and bottom, make the top and bottom slightly shorter and rabbet the joints. If you dado grooves in the sides instead of nailing the shelf, make the shelf slightly longer.

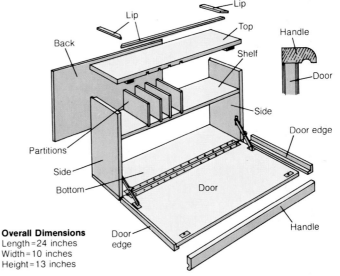

Overall Dimensions
Length = 24 inches
Width = 10 inches
Height = 13 inches

LUMBER TO BUY		MILL TO	FOR PROJECT PIECE
Birch (FAS grade)			
1	1" × 12" × 8'	2 ¾" × 10" × 24"	Top and bottom
		1 ¾" × 9¾" × 22½"	Shelf
		2 ¾" × 10" × 11½"	Sides
		2 ¾" × 1" × 11½"	Door edging
		1 ¼" × ⅜" × 22"	Lips
		2 ¼" × ⅜" × 9"	
Walnut (FAS grade)			
1	1" × 2" × 2'	1 ¾" × 1¾" × 24"	Handle
Birch plywood			
1	¾" × 1' × 2'	1 ¾" × 11½" × 24"	Door
1	¼" × 1' × 3'	1 ¼" × 12½" × 23½"	Back
		4 ¼" × 4½" × 9¾"	Partitions

Hardware & Miscellaneous	
6d finishing nails	2 lid-support hinges
½" brads	2 magnetic catches
2' piano hinge	Glue

FILING-CABINET DESK

The desk is easy to build because it consists mainly of a ready-made hollow-core door faced with plastic laminate, and its pedestals are metal filing cabinets. The optional cubbyhole case is a bit more complex, but well worth the effort. It is most effective if hung on the wall about a foot above the desk surface.

DESK-TOP CONSTRUCTION

Step 1. Mill the walnut edging.

Step 2. Spread contact cement on the door with a spreading tool or paint roller, set the plastic laminate onto the door so all the edges are covered, and press it down firmly.

Step 3. When the cement has set, trim the plastic flush with the door (see page 92).

Step 4. Pre-sand the walnut edging before attaching it to the door to avoid scratching the plastic.

Step 5. Glue and nail the edging to the door flush with the plastic surface.

Step 6. Set the nails, fill the holes, and finish the edging.

Step 7. Position the file cabinets and lay the top in place.

CUBBYHOLE-CASE CONSTRUCTION

Step 1. Mill the top, bottom, ends, and full-height vertical partitions, and rip the ¼-inch by ½-inch edge strips.

Step 2. Cut out, glue, and nail the two 10½-inch corner edge trims to the tops of the two ends.

Step 3. Follow the illustration and dado grooves for the shelves and partitions in the top, bottom, ends, and full-height partitions. These should be ½-inch wide to accommodate the ½-inch plywood, and 5/32-inch deep.

Step 4. Assemble the top, bottom, ends

LUMBER TO BUY	MILL TO		FOR PROJECT PIECE
Walnut (FAS grade)			
3 1"× 3"× 6'	2	¾"× 2"× 72"	Edging
	2	¾"× 2"× 32"	

Hardware & Miscellaneous	
1 32"× 70½" hollow-core door	Contact cement
1 3'× 6' plastic laminate sheet (Formica, etc.)	Wood putty
	Glue
6d finishing nails	

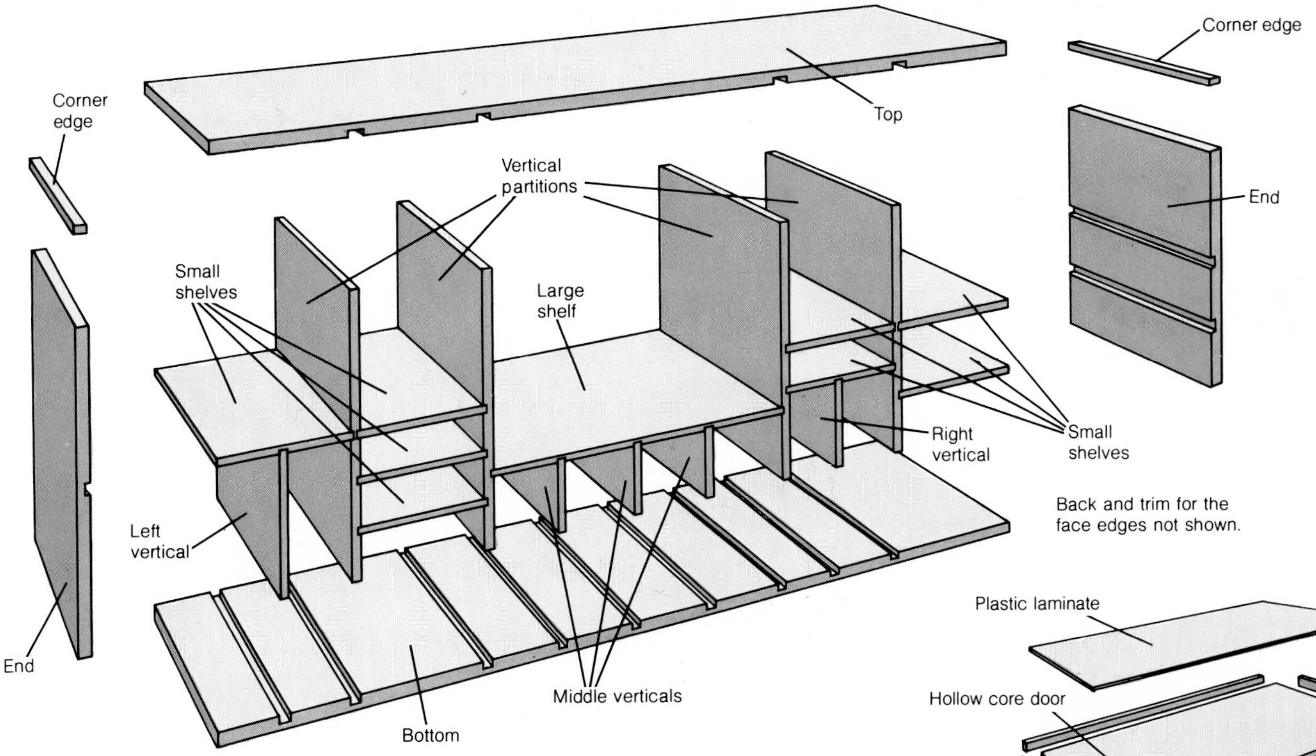
Corner edge
Top
Corner edge
End
Vertical partitions
Small shelves
Large shelf
Right vertical
Small shelves
Left vertical
End
Middle verticals
Bottom
Back and trim for the face edges not shown.

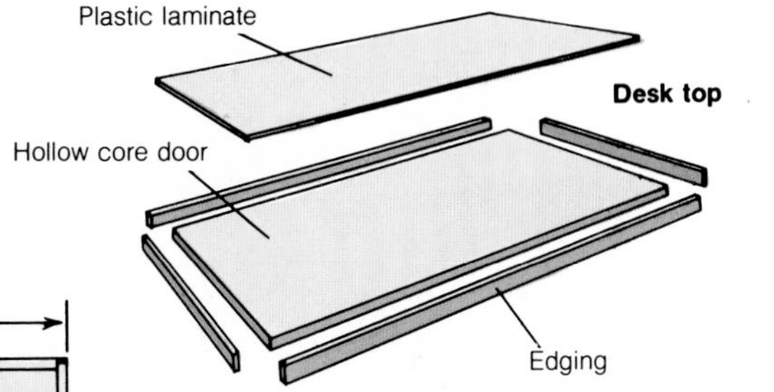
Plastic laminate
Desk top
Hollow core door
Edging

Overall Dimensions
Length=72 inches
Width=33½ inches

Dimensions between shelf and partition dadoes

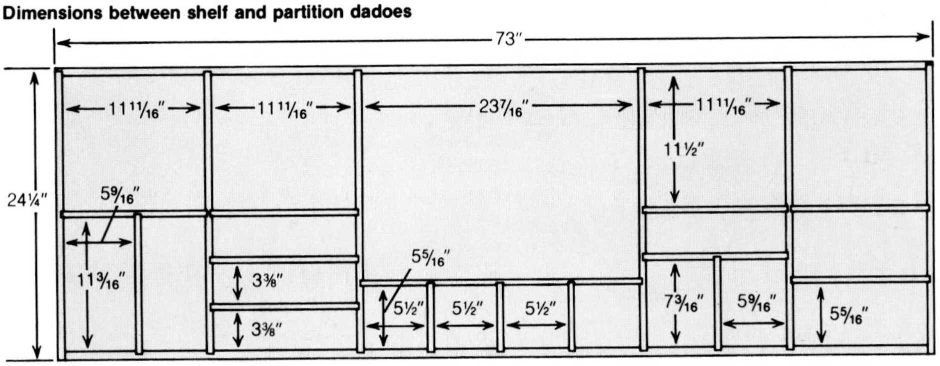
73″
24¼″
11¹¹⁄₁₆″
11¹¹⁄₁₆″
23⁷⁄₁₆″
11¹¹⁄₁₆″
11½″
5⁹⁄₁₆″
11³⁄₁₆″
3⅜″
3⅜″
5⁵⁄₁₆″
5½″
5½″
5½″
7³⁄₁₆″
5⁹⁄₁₆″
5⁵⁄₁₆″

and partitions with glue and 1-inch brads, making sure they are square.

Step 5. After checking measurements, mill the back and nail it with 1-inch brads to the top, bottom, sides, and partitions.

Step 6. Check measurements for the remaining shelves and partitions and mill them.

Step 7. Dado grooves ½-inch by 5⁄32 inch in the three shelves that rest above vertical partitions, and slide the shelves and partitions into place.

Step 8. Cut out and sand all the face trims, and glue and nail them onto the front edges of all the plywood with ½-inch brads. Then set the nails and fill the holes.

Step 9. Finish the case as desired, then hang it on the wall or place it on top of the desk.

LUMBER TO BUY	MILL TO		FOR PROJECT PIECE
Walnut plywood			
1 ½″×4′×8′	2	½″×10½″×72″	Top and bottom
	2	½″×10½″×24″	Ends
	4	½″×10″×23½″	Vertical partitions
	8	½″×10″×12″	Small shelves
	1	½″×10″×23¾″	Large shelf
	1	½″×10″×11½″	Left vertical
	1	½″×10″×7½″	Right vertical
	3	½″×10″×5⅝″	Middle verticals
1 ¼″×4′×8′	1	¼″×23″×72″	Back
Walnut (FAS grade)			
1 1″×2″×7′	24	¼″×½″ strips:	Edge trim
	2	¼″×½″×10½″	Corner edges
	2	¼″×½″×73″	Face edges
	6	¼″×½″×23″	
	8	¼″×½″×11¹¹⁄₁₆″	
	1	¼″×½″×11⁵⁄₁₆″	
	1	¼″×½″×7⁵⁄₁₆″	
	3	¼″×½″×5⁵⁄₁₆″	
	1	¼″×½″×23⁹⁄₁₆″	

Hardware & Miscellaneous	
½″ brads	Wood putty
1″ brads	Glue

CORNER DESK

For this desk we used nominal stock, so it's simple to build. It will fit where other desks won't, and the shelves can be turned toward the knee space to accommodate bordering furniture. And perhaps best of all, it can grow with its user. By reducing the height of the cases it is good for a child; later you can add pedestals and raise the nailers to make the desk taller.

MATERIALS TO BUY	MILL TO			FOR PROJECT PIECE
Particle board				
1″ × 4′ × 4′	1	1″ × 40½″ × 40½″		Top
Pine (grade A or B select)				
1 1″ × 4″ × 6′	2	¾″ × 3½″ × 11″		Edging
	1	¾″ × 3½″ × 43″		
2 1″ × 10″ × 8′	4	¾″ × 9¼″ × 29¼″		Sides
	4	¾″ × 9¼″ × 9″		Tops and bottoms
	4	¾″ × 9¼″ × 8¾″		Shelves
1 1″ × 3″ × 6′	2	¾″ × 2¾″ × 9″		Toes
	2	¾″ × 2¾″ × 24″		Wall nailers
1 ½″ × 4″ × 6′	2	½″ × 2½″ × 22″		Drawer sides
	1	½″ × 2″ × 22″		Drawer back
Fir plywood or hardboard				
1 ¼″ × 4′ × 4′	1	¼″ × 23½″ × 22¼″		Drawer bottom
	2	¼″ × 9½″ × 26″		Base backs
Plastic laminate (Formica, etc.)				
1 4′ × 4′	1	41″ × 41″		Top

Hardware & Miscellaneous	
6d finishing nails	Contact cement
16 shelf-support clips	Wood putty
1 pair drawer slides	Glue

CONSTRUCTION

Step 1. Mill the particle-board top, marking the line for the angle by measuring 10½ inches in from the corners.

Step 2. Cut the plastic laminate several inches larger than you need it and glue it to the particle board with contact cement. Press it down firmly and allow the glue to dry.

Step 3. Trim the laminate flush with the particle board (see page 92).

Step 4. Mill the edging, mitering one end of each small piece and both ends of the large piece 22½ degrees.

Step 5. Cut a drawer front 2½ inches by 24 inches out of the large edging (see page 86).

Step 6. Mill the remaining drawer pieces and assemble the drawer (see page 91). Be sure to leave clearance for the drawer slides (usually 1 inch) as indicated in the manufacturer's instructions, and install the drawer as directed.

Step 7. Mill the tops, bottoms, sides, shelves, and backs for the bases.

Step 8. Cut rabbets ¼-inch wide in the back edges of the tops, bottoms, and sides to accept the backs (see page 87).

Step 9. Drill holes in the sides for the adjustable-shelf clips (see page 91).

Step 10. Assemble the bases with glue and nails. Set the nails and fill the holes.

Step 11. Sand and finish as desired.

Step 12. Mount nailers to the wall 29¼ inches from the floor (see drawing).

Step 13. Set the top onto the bases and wall nailers, insert the adjustable shelves, and your desk is finished.

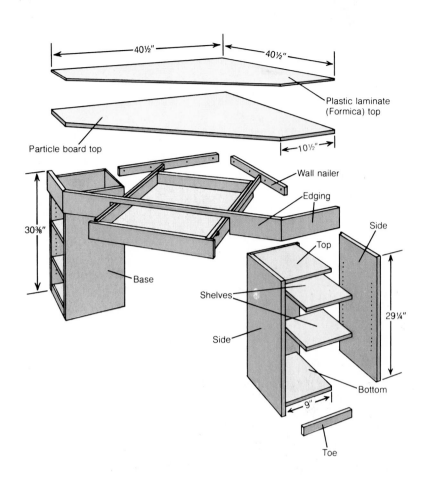

SANDWICH DESK

This commodious desk for home or office can be built easily by following the instructions for the modular units given in the living and dining room chapter. Build and assemble a set of sandwich drawers, two basic chests with doors or drawers, and two high pedestals. Set them together and you have the desk shown in the photograph.

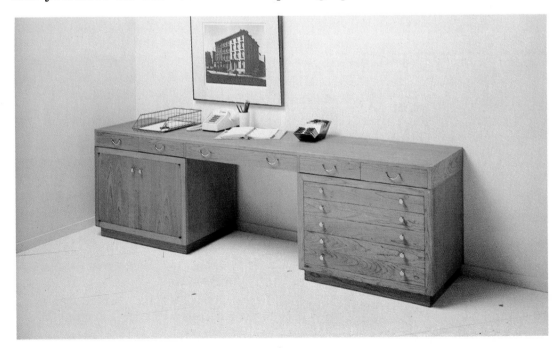

SPORTS STORAGE

These storage units are ideal for outsized equipment, clothing, and footwear that are often too bulky or muddy for a regular closet. Each has a clothes pole and two shelves—one adjustable—and a tall, narrow equipment compartment. We recommend building a separate unit for each family member, or one for each sport. Our materials list covers one unit.

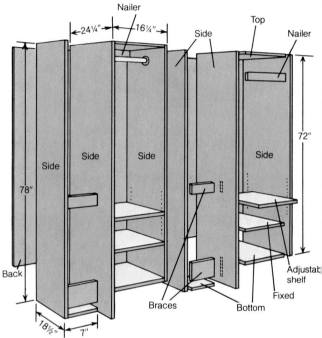

CONSTRUCTION

Step 1. Mill all the pieces.

Step 2. Measure for and drill the ¼-inch holes for the adjustable-shelf clips in all the 24-inch sides.

Step 3. Glue and nail the 15-inch tops and bottoms, the fixed shelves, and the 15-inch nailers between the 24-inch sides.

Step 4. Glue and nail the 7⅛-inch bottoms, braces, and nailers between the 24-inch sides and the 18-inch sides.

Step 5. Turn each unit over and attach the plywood backs with glue and box nails. (Place several 6-inch blocks beneath the 18-inch sides to hold them at the same height as the 24-inch sides.)

Step 6. Set all the nails, fill the holes, and sand and paint the units.

Step 7. Install the clothes poles and adjustable shelves.

Step 8. Attach the units to a convenient basement or garage wall, using molly bolts or lag screws.

LUMBER TO BUY	MILL TO		FOR PROJECT PIECE
Plywood (grade AB)			
2 ⅝″× 4′× 8′	1	⅝″× 24″× 78″	Sides
	1	⅝″× 24″× 72″	
	1	⅝″× 18″× 78″	
	2	⅝″× 24″× 15″	Top and bottom
	1	⅝″× 18″× 7⅛″	Fixed shelf
	1	⅝″× 24″× 14¾″	Adjustable shelf
	1	⅝″× 3″× 15″	Braces and nailers
	2	⅝″× 3″× 7⅛″	
	1	⅝″× 6″× 7⅛″	
Plywood (grade AD)			
1 ¼″× 2′× 8′	1	¼″× 24″× 72″	Back
Dowel			
1 1¼″ dia.× 2′	1	1¼″ dia.× 14½″	Clothes pole

Hardware & Miscellaneous	
1 pair clothes-pole brackets	6d box nails
4 shelf clips	Wood putty
6d finishing nails	Glue

BATHROOM STORAGE

This provides extra storage and makes your bathroom look bigger, with minimal effort. It is built of nominal wood that you just cut to length, so it's very easy to assemble. The mirror and glass shelves give it a light line and open look, and there's closed storage too. Use whatever wood you like, and dress it however you'd like.

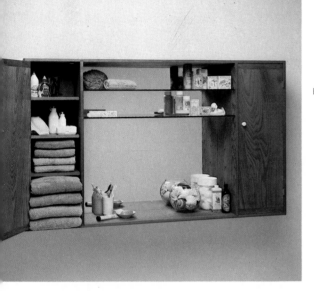

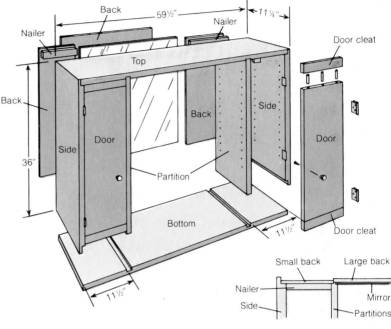

Detail of Rabbets and how mirror backs fit into them

CONSTRUCTION

Step 1. Mill all the lumber.

Step 2. Dowel and glue the cleats to the ends of each door (see page 89) and set aside to dry.

Step 3. Where the ends of the sides join the top and bottom, cut rabbets in the sides ¾-inch deep by ½-inch wide (see page 87).

Step 4. For the partitions in the top and bottom, dado grooves ¼-inch deep by ¾-inch wide, 11¾ inches from the ends.

Step 5. Cut ½-inch deep rabbets in the top, bottom, and sides for the backs and the mirror, and ⅛-inch deep rabbets in the partitions (see drawing).

Step 6. Drill holes for shelf clips in the sides and partitions (see page 89) for the glass shelves and the adjustable wooden cabinet shelves.

Step 7. Assemble the top, bottom, sides, and partitions with glue and nails; set the nails and fill the holes with wood putty.

Step 8. Nail the small backs into place and install a nailer at the top of each side, as shown.

Step 9. Clean, sand, and finish the case, doors, and wooden shelves.

Step 10. Install the doors, catches, and wooden shelves.

Step 11. Install the mirror and carefully nail the large plywood back over it to hold it in place.

Step 12. Mount the unit to the wall by nailing into studs through the nailers at the top of each side, or by using molly bolts.

Step 13. Insert the glass shelves.

LUMBER TO BUY		MILL TO		FOR PROJECT PIECE
Redwood (grade A select)				
3	1"× 12"× 12'	2	¾"× 11¼"× 59¼"	Top and bottom
		2	¾"× 11¼"× 36"	Sides
		2	¾"× 10⅞"× 35"	Partitions
		4	¾"× 10⅛"× 11"	Shelves
		2	¾"× 11¼"× 32"	Doors
1	1"× 2"× 4'	4	¾"× 1¾"× 11¼"	Door cleats
		2	¾"× 1¾"× 11¼"	Nailers
Fir plywood				
1	¼"× 4'× 4'	2	¼"× 12"× 35¼"	Backs
		1	¼"× 35½"× 35¼"	

Hardware & Miscellaneous	
12 ⅜" dia.× 2½" grooved dowels	2 door pulls
24 shelf-support clips	2 door catches
6d finishing nails	4 2" butt hinges
⅛" single-strength mirror 35½"× 35¼"	Wood putty
2 34½"× 10½" plate-glass shelves	Glue

CELLAR WINE STORAGE

For the serious collector or winemaker who wants to store many bottles in a cellar for long periods of time, this rack is perfect. Redwood or cedar is recommended to withstand the dampness of cellars, and legs and feet will add stability on an uneven floor. Or, if your ceiling has open floor-joists, you can attach the rack to the ceiling with cleats.

CONSTRUCTION

Step 1. Cut stock to size.

Step 2. Draw a center line the length of the 1 by 6 boards, which will become the front stringers. Mark each center line 4 inches from one end and then every 3½ inches. The twelfth mark should be 4 inches from the other end.

Step 3. With a hole saw, cut a 1½-inch hole at the exact center of each of these marks.

Step 4. Rip the 1 by 6 boards in half so you have ten 1 by 3 front stringers, each with 12 semicircular cutouts evenly spaced along one edge.

Step 5. To begin work on the back stringers, draw a line ¾ inch from the edge down the length of one of the (uncut) 1 by 3s. Mark center lines on this line as instructed in step 2.

Step 6. Cut a 4-inch circle from a piece of cardboard or find a cup or jar lid that is close to 4 inches in diameter. As illustrated, center the circle on each of the marks and draw the part of the circle that fits in the ¾-inch area between the line and the edge of the board.

Step 7. Cut the 12 arcs with a saber, jig, or band saw. The board will match the front stringers, but will have larger scallops.

Step 8. Trace the large scallops onto the nine remaining back stringers and saw these arcs too.

Step 9. Dado notches on the front and back of each side piece. These are to be ⅜-inch deep and as wide as the front and back stringers. The lowest one starts 4⅜ inches above the bottom and they are spaced 6½ inches on center.

Step 10. Draw all the cutting lines on the legs (see illustration); a 10-degree angle at the top on each side, and a 1-inch by 7½-inch cutout at the bottom (giving them a 2½-inch foot at each end).

Step 11. Drill two ⅜-inch holes 2 inches deep through each of these feet, as illustrated. Drive a glue-covered dowel into each hole, and after the glue has set saw them off flush with the bottom of the feet. These will prevent the feet from splitting if the rack is dragged on the floor.

Step 12. Cut the legs, using a power saw for the angles and a hand saw and chisel for the cutout between the feet.

Step 13. Dado a notch in the legs and across the bottom of the side pieces where they join, cutting ⅛ inch less than halfway through. This will cause the leg to protrude ¼ inch from the side piece—a nice detail.

Step 14. Hold each leg in position on each side piece and drill two ¼-inch holes through both at once. Set the legs aside.

Step 15. Prefinish the stringers before assembling the rack.

Step 16. Check whether the assembled rack will fit through your doorways. If not, assemble it in your cellar.

Step 17. Attach the front stringers. Lay the sides on edge and lay the stringers in the dadoed notches. Drill two ¹⁄₁₆-inch pilot holes through the end of each stringer and screw them on.

Step 18. Turn the rack over and attach the back stringers the same way.

Step 19. Attach the legs with the four carriage bolts, washers, and nuts.

Step 20. Raise the rack, and sand and finish as desired.

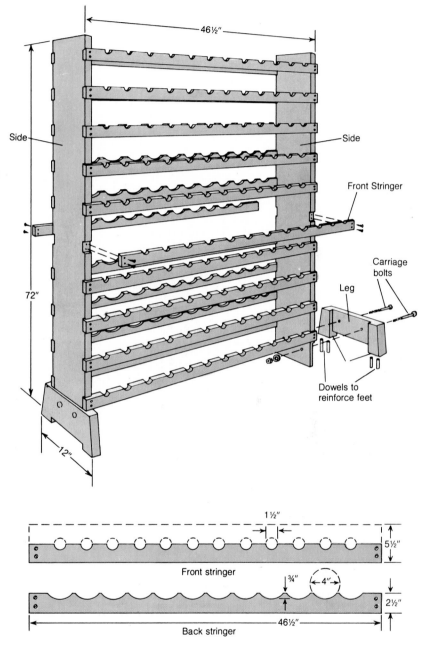

LUMBER TO BUY		MILL TO		FOR PROJECT PIECE
Redwood (grade AB select)				
2	2″× 8″× 6′	2	1½″× 7¼″× 72″	Sides
		2	1½″× 7¼″× 12″	Legs
5	1″× 6″× 4′	5	¾″× 5½″× 46½″	Front stringers
10	1″× 3″× 4′	10	¾″× 2½″× 46½″	Back stringers

Hardware & Miscellaneous	
80 1½″× #8 round-head brass wood screws	4 ¼″× 2″ carriage bolts; washers; nuts
	4 ⅜″× 2½″ grooved dowels

CEDAR CHEST

Now, this is a chest—beautiful, and supplying plenty of room. You'll love the smell of the incense cedar—perhaps especially because insects don't, and they'll stay far away. To keep them away, finish only the outside so as not to diminish the fragrance. Instead of countersinking and plugging the screws, you may want to use brass screws and allow them to show.

CONSTRUCTION

Step 1. Mill all the pieces. To make the lid slats fit snugly over the curve of the top, set the saw blade at a 4½-degree angle when you rip the 1 by 6s. Bevel each edge so the bottom of each slat is narrower than the 1¾-inch top (see illustration).

Step 2. For the lid supports, center the 20-inch pieces on the 23½-inch pieces, glue and clamp them together, and set them aside to dry.

Step 3. To build each side, place the two corner braces 24 inches apart and lay the side pieces on top of them flush with the top edges and sides of the braces. Attach each board to the braces with two 1½-inch screws at each end. Use a drill and counterbore bit to make a pilot hole for the screw and a hole for the plug (see page 89).

Step 4. Assemble the front and back by attaching the pieces to the center brace so the tops are flush, using countersunk 1¼-inch screws.

Step 5. Partially assemble the chest by screwing the front and back to the sides, countersinking two 1½-inch screws through each board into the corner braces. The front and back should overlap the sides.

Step 6. Assemble the bottom braces with glue and two grooved dowels in each joint. Allow to set.

Step 7. Use 6-penny finishing nails to attach the bottom boards to the bottom bracing flush with the edges.

Step 8. Turn the chest upside down to attach the bottom by countersinking three 1½-inch screws through both the front and back into the bracing, and two through each side.

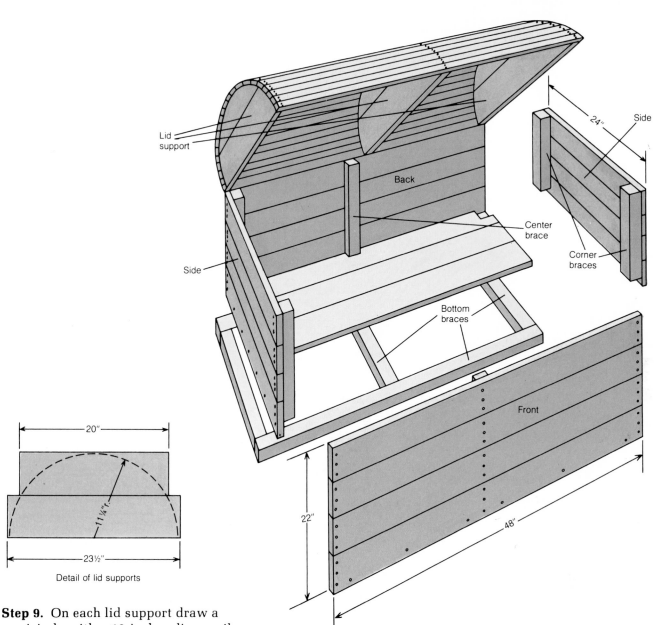

Lid support

Back

Center brace

Side

24"

Side

Corner braces

Bottom braces

Front

22"

48"

20"

11¼"

23½"

Detail of lid supports

Step 9. On each lid support draw a semicircle with a 12-inch radius, as illustrated, and cut them out.

Step 10. Assemble the lid with six countersunk #8 screws per slat (two per support). Screw the first slat flush over the bottom of each end and then the center, and continue working around the semicircle. Adjust the width of the last slat if necessary before screwing it to the top.

Step 11. Cut enough plugs from scrap cedar (see page 89) to cover all the screws, and glue them in place. Use a damp cloth to remove excess glue as you proceed, and when the glue has set chisel the plugs flush.

Step 12. Attach the lid to the chest with the piano hinge and brass chain, and attach the remaining hardware as shown in the photograph.

LUMBER TO BUY	MILL TO		PROJECT PIECE
Incense cedar (grade C select)			
15 1"× 6"× 8'	8	¾"× 5¾"× 48"	Front and back
	8	¾"× 5¾"× 24"	Sides
	5	¾"× 5¾"× 46½"	Bottom
	3	¾"× 5¾"× 23½"	Lid supports
	3	¾"× 5¾"× 20"	
	21	¾"× 1¾"× 48"	Lid slats
Mahogany (FAS grade)			
7 2"× 2"× 4'	4	1¾"× 1¾"× 19"	Corner braces
	2	1¾"× 1¾"× 46½"	Bottom braces
	3	1¾"× 1¾"× 20½"	
	2	¾"× 1¾"× 19"	Center braces

Hardware & Miscellaneous	
126 1½"× #8 flat-head wood screws	4 brass screw eyes
96 1½"× #10 flat-head wood screws	3' brass sash chain
24 1¼"× #10 flat-head wood screws	2 brass handles
12 ⅜" dia.× 2½" grooved dowel plugs	1 brass hasp
6d finishing nails	1 brass padlock
48" brass piano hinge	Glue

CHILDREN'S CENTER

This storage and play group has a place for just about everything: open shelves for display, a closed cabinet for storage, and a desk connection between them. The desk has large cubbyholes for drawing paper as well as small drawers, and for smaller children a work table and sitting bench can be tucked underneath it. You can raise the desk as needed to adapt the center to kids of all ages.

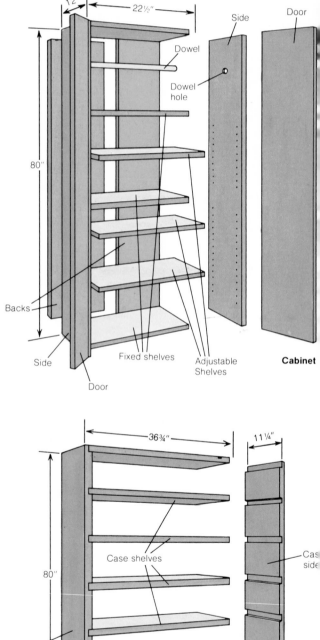

Cabinet

BOOK/DISPLAY-CASE CONSTRUCTION

Step 1. Mill all the pieces.

Step 2. Dado seven ¾-inch grooves ³⁄₁₆-inch deep across the sides where the shelves will join, and a ¾-inch by ³⁄₁₆-inch rabbet at the top for the top shelf.

Step 3. Glue and nail the shelves into the grooves and rabbet.

CABINET CONSTRUCTION

Step 1. Mill all the pieces.
Step 2. Drill ¼-inch holes for the adjustable shelves in the sides (see page 89), and a 1-inch hole in the center of both sides for the dowel rod (see illustration).

Step 3. Use a framing square and assemble the top, bottom, sides, and fixed shelves with glue and nails, and insert the 1-inch dowel.

Step 4. Fit the two back pieces in place and attach with glue and nails.

Step 5. Attach the doors with hinges.

Step 6. Insert the adjustable shelves.

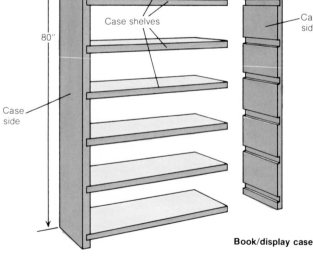

Book/display case

DESK CONSTRUCTION

Step 1. Mill all but the drawer pieces.

Step 2. As illustrated, dado ¾-inch grooves ³⁄₁₆-inch deep in the middle of the verticals to house the horizontal pieces.

Step 3. Glue and nail the verticals to the bottom and the top to the verticals, and glue the horizontals between the verticals. Use a framing square to assure accuracy.

Step 4. Measure the drawer openings and mill the drawer pieces to fit. Assemble the drawers following one of the methods on page 91.

TABLE AND BENCH CONSTRUCTION

Step 1. Mill all the pieces.

Step 2. Glue and nail the end skirt-pieces to the side skirts so the sides overlap the ends.

Step 3. Drill pilot holes and counterbore for ½-inch screw plugs in the ends of the skirts (see page 89). Glue and screw the legs into the corners ¾ inch below the top of the skirts.

Step 4 (table only). Glue and nail the 1 by 3 brace to the end skirts ¾ inch below the top.

Step 5. Drop the top inside the skirt so it rests on top of the legs, and nail it in place with finishing nails. Then set the nails.

Step 6. Glue dowel plugs into the ½-inch holes or fill the holes with wood putty; fill the nail holes in the top.

ASSEMBLY

Step 1. Finish each piece. Set nails and fill holes, then clean, sand, mount magnetic catches to each side of the cabinet and doors, mount all door and drawer pulls, and seal.

Step 2. Raise and hold the desk against the side of the cabinet (using saw horses or a friend) so its top is 28 to 30 inches from the floor. Drill two ¼-inch holes through the sides of both, making sure you drill into the empty cubbyholes rather than into the desk drawers. Then drill into the book/display case on the other side.

Step 3. Secure the desk between the cabinet and the case with stove bolts, washers, and nuts.

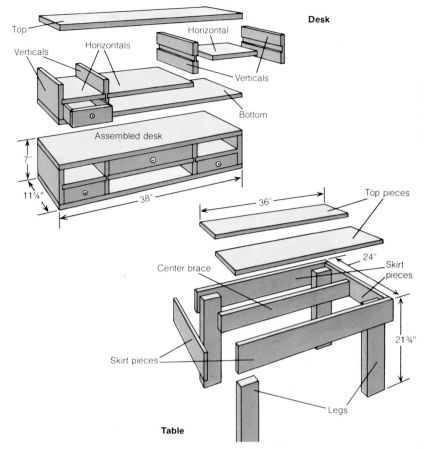

LUMBER TO BUY		MILL TO		FOR PROJECT PIECE
Pine (grades B and C select)				
10	1"×12"×8'	4	¾"×11¼"×80"	Cabinet and case sides
		2	¾"×11¼"×78"	Cabinet doors
		2	¾"×10½"×76½"	Cabinet back
		2	¾"×11¼"×38"	Desk top and bottom
		4	¾"×11¼"×5½"	Desk verticals
		2	¾"×11¼"×9⅝"	Desk horizontals
		1	¾"×11¼"×16⅝"	
5	1"×12"×10'	8	¾"×11¼"×36"	Case shelves
		2	¾"×11¼"×21"	Cabinet top and bottom
		2	¾"×10¼"×21"	Cabinet fixed-shelves
		6	¾"×10¼"×20¾"	Cabinet adjustable-shelves
		2	¾"×11¼"×34½"	Table top
		1	¾"×11¼"×28½"	Bench top
1	1"×4"×10'	2	¾"×3½"×36"	Table skirt
		2	¾"×3½"×22½"	
1	1"×4"×8'	2	¾"×3½"×30"	Bench skirt
		2	¾"×3½"×11¼"	
1	2"×4"×8'	4	1½"×3½"×21"	Table legs
1	2"×4"×6'	4	1½"×3½"×12"	Bench legs
1	1"×3"×10'	2	¾"×2⅜"×9¼"	Drawer fronts
		1	¾"×2⅜"×16¼"	
		2	¾"×1⅞"×9¼"	Drawer backs
		1	¾"×1⅞"×16¼"	
		1	¾"×2⅜"×34½"	Table center brace
1	½"×3"×6'	6	½"×2⅜"×10½"	Drawer sides

Hardware & Miscellaneous

32 1½"× #8 flat-head wood screws	24 shelf clips
32 ½" dowel plugs (optional)	2 magnetic catches
4 ¼" dia.× 1½" flat-head stove bolts; washers; nuts	5 drawer/door pulls
	3' 1" dia. doweling
6d finishing nails	Wood putty
2 pair cabinet door hinges	Glue

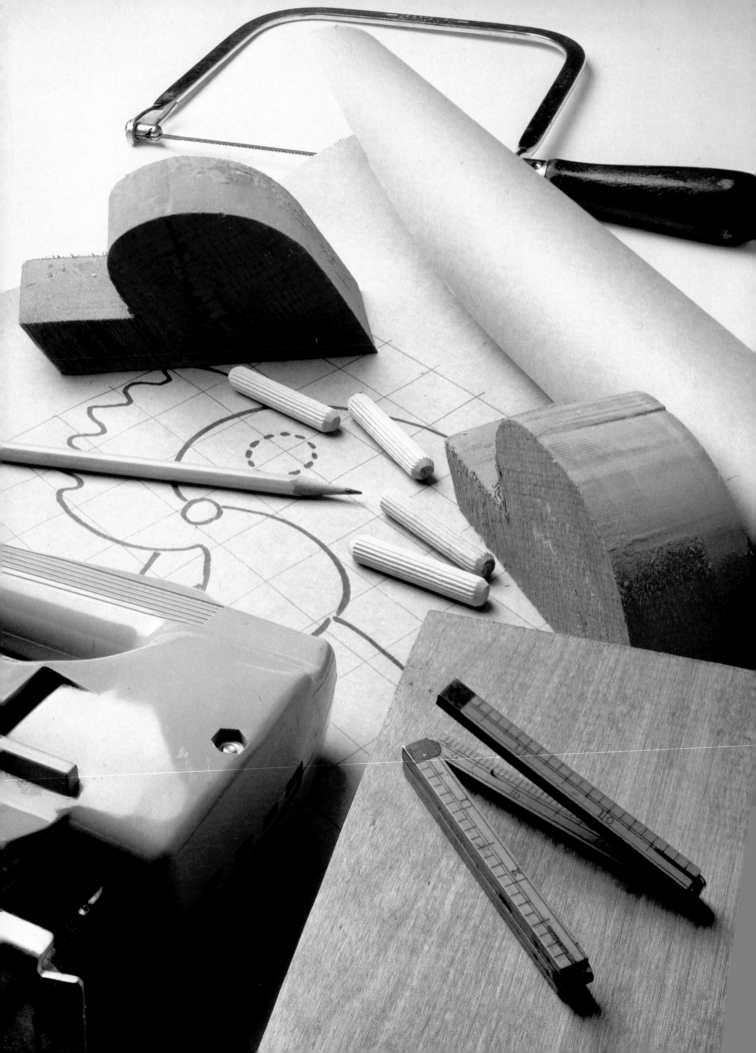

• CHILDREN'S FURNITURE & TOYS •

There is a wonderful feeling of sharing when you build toys and furniture for children. Here are some projects that can be built in an hour or a few days: building blocks, coat rack, bulletin board, bed, easel, doll house, teeter totter, toy chest, and rocking horse. Each one is satisfying for the builder and a delight for the child.

Woodworking projects are often initiated by the very practical needs of growing children. Whether it is a simple set of shelves to hold treasures or an entire room full of furniture, every project provides both adults and children with a special sort of sharing and makes each particularly fun to build.

Like all of our projects, these can be easily altered, and many can be made for adults as well. For example, the coat rack can be dressed up with fancy pegs to suit a front entry; the chest can store anything; and the bed will work equally well on a king-sized scale.

Our blocks were made largely of walnut scraps, which made them as beautiful as they are durable. This is a good beginning project for practicing measuring and cutting, and for getting to know the qualities of different woods.

The bulletin board can be made with a minimum of tools, for use anywhere. This is a good project to play with for practicing miter cuts and shaping molding, and will prepare you for the mirror frame in the living and dining room chapter.

The two-sided easel is a perfect rainy-day or any-day gift for a child, especially because it can be used with a playmate. The trays are big enough to hold lots of crayons and paints, and the hardboard faces are designed to hold large pads of paper. The easel is sturdy yet portable, as it comes apart and can be folded flat for storage or transport.

Children particularly love the doll house because of its easy access for play. Building it takes less than a day, but it will keep your children happy for years!

The toy chest is a snap to assemble with fir tongue-and-groove flooring. Just cut the flooring and braces to length and get out your glue, hammer, and nails, and in a couple of hours you can say goodbye to tripping over toys. Brass hardware adds a nice finishing touch, and adjustable-tension lid supports make the chest safe for children to use.

Two-year olds can mount our indoor teeter totter all by themselves, and it won't tip over when it is ridden alone. It's also sturdy enough to be ridden by grownups!

The beautiful bed we made for one of our children can be built with equal effect for the largest adults. It is an especially elegant bed if it is made with fine wood.

The last project in this book—a wonderful, whimsical rocking horse—is really quite special and unlike any of the others. To build it, three qualities are probably essential: the courage to try something different, a bit of imagination to sculpt the design, and strength to handle the lumber. Skilled use of a chain saw will help in the building, and skilled use of diplomacy will help in the placement—for everyone in your household may well want to fight for this horse!

COAT RACK

Here is a simple, nice way to hang coats on the wall. The rack can be made with dowels and painted for a kids' room or back entry, or more elegantly, with turned pegs and a fine finish.

CONSTRUCTION

Step 1. Mark centers of dowel or peg placements. They should all be aligned about ½ inch above the horizontal center-line of the board, and 6 inches apart.

Step 2. Drill 1-inch holes for the pegs as illustrated. Hold the drill plumb as you bore the holes.

Step 3 (optional). Shape the front edges of the board with a router (see page 88). Pre-sand the board before gluing pegs.

Step 4. Spread a bead of glue around the bottom edge of each peg and push the pegs into the holes. Let the glue dry.

Step 5. Sand and finish as desired (see page 93).

MATERIALS TO BUY

1 2″× 6″× 32″ scrap lumber
1 1″ dia.× 4′ dowel (cut 5 pegs 6″ long)
Glue

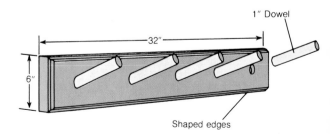

1″ Dowel

32″

6″

Shaped edges

Step 2. Prop top edge of board on 2-inch scrap. Hold drill plumb.

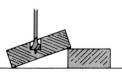

BULLETIN BOARD

Feel free to use these instructions to make bulletin boards of any size—for your child's room, a home office, the end of a cabinet—with a minimum of tools. Buy picture-frame molding, or make your own frame with a dado set and power saw, or shaping bits and a router. Then embellish it with different colors of paint.

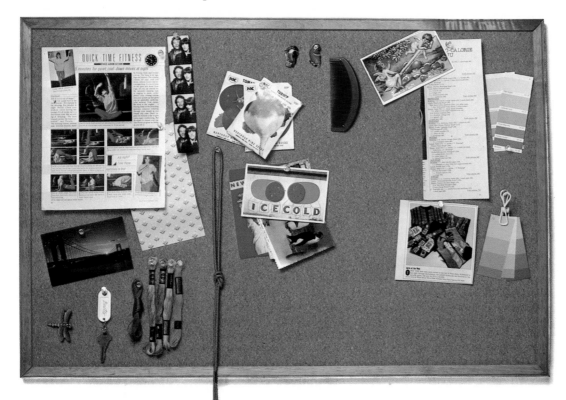

CONSTRUCTION

Step 1. Spread the plywood or hardboard backing with cork adhesive, then apply the cork and smooth it out. Let the adhesive dry.

Step 2. From the back, trim any edges where the cork overhangs the backing.

Step 3. Miter-cut the molding to length and set it in place on the cork to be sure it fits exactly.

Step 4. Paint, stain, or otherwise prefinish the molding.

Step 5. When the finish is dry, glue and nail the molding to the edges of the cork and backing. Nail the corners of the molding if necessary, then set the nails and fill the holes.

Step 6. Affix two sawtooth hangers to the back of the molding and put nails in the wall.

MATERIALS TO BUY

1 2'× 3' sheet of cork or Celotex	2 sawtooth adjustable picture hangers
1 2'× 3' sheet of ¼" plywood or hardboard	Cork adhesive and spreading tool
2 6' strips of bulletin-board or picture-frame molding	Wood putty

BLOCKS

Kids of all ages love blocks, and they're a perfect use for scrap lumber. We made ours of doweling and pieces of walnut and cherry. Cut the scraps in a variety of sizes, sand them well, and rub them with nontoxic mineral oil.

EASEL

Delight your child with a place to dream up a world—with room for a playmate. This two-sided easel is designed to have the hardboard faces extend over the top, so you can easily clip on large pads of paper. And it comes apart and folds flat for storage or transport. We chose hardwood for its weight and to minimize chips and dents; you may use any wood.

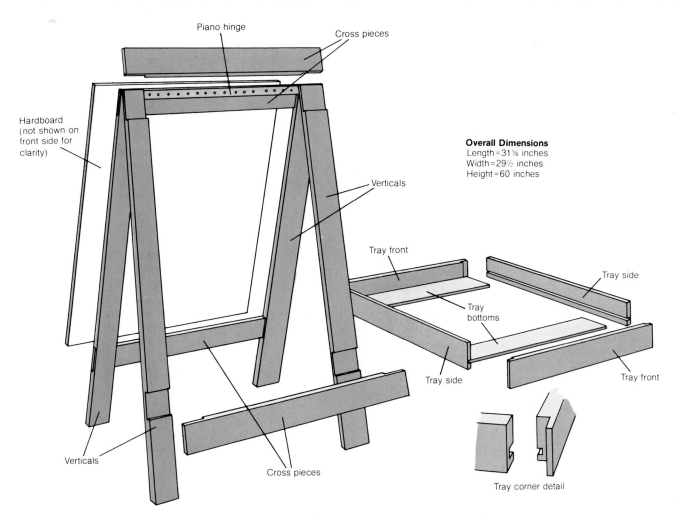

Piano hinge

Cross pieces

Hardboard (not shown on front side for clarity)

Verticals

Overall Dimensions
Length = 31⅝ inches
Width = 29½ inches
Height = 60 inches

Tray front

Tray bottoms

Tray side

Verticals

Tray side

Tray front

Cross pieces

Tray corner detail

CONSTRUCTION

Step 1. Mill the lumber and hardboard.

Step 2. Dado the lap joints for the verticals and cross-pieces (see page 87). The lower edge of the bottom cross-piece should be 12¾ inches from the bottom of the verticals.

Step 3. Glue and clamp the verticals and cross-pieces together and set them aside to dry.

Step 4. Dado a ¼-inch slot for the hardboard ¼ inch from the bottom of all four tray pieces.

Step 5. Rabbet the ends of the tray fronts to accept the tray sides. Cut the rabbet the width of the side and ⅝-inch deep, leaving ⅛ inch of front to overlap the end grain of the sides (see page 87).

Step 6. Glue and nail the tray together with the hardboard bottoms in place.

Step 7. When the glue is dry, lay the two big frames head-to-head and join them together with the piano hinge.

Step 8. Fold the frames together and screw the hardboard to each side. Set the bottom of the hardboard flush with the bottom edge of the lower cross-piece.

The hardboard should extend above the top cross-piece by ¾ inch.

Step 9. Set the tray over the frame and prop it (or have a friend hold it) even with the bottom of the hardboard, and spread the frame to touch the tray bottoms. Drill a 1/16-inch pilot hole through the tray into the side of each frame leg. Put a round-head screw with a washer into each hole and tighten them. These screws can be removed so you can store or transport the easel.

Step 10. Clean, sand, and paint or stain as you wish.

MATERIALS TO BUY		MILL TO		FOR PROJECT PIECE
Birch (FAS grade)				
3	1″ × 3″ × 10′	4	¾″ × 2½″ × 60″	Verticals
		4	¾″ × 2½″ × 30″	Cross pieces
		2	¾″ × 2½″ × 31⅝″	Tray fronts
		2	¾″ × 2½″ × 28″	Tray sides
Masonite (hardboard)				
1	¼″ × 4′ × 8′	2	¼″ × 48″ × 30″	Faces
		2	¼″ × 4¼″ × 30½″	Tray bottoms

Hardware & Miscellaneous	
1 30″ piano hinge	26 ¾″ × #8 flat-head wood screws
4 2″ × #8 round-head wood screws; washers	4 large spring clips
	Glue

DOLL HOUSE

This is the doll house of dreams, and a chance to give a child years of pleasure from a half-day's work. It is scaled to accommodate ready-made furniture, tall enough to be played with comfortably, and much sturdier than commercial doll houses. This is one to hand down for years—if its first owner will ever part with it.

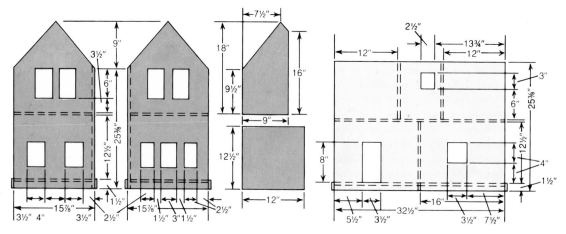

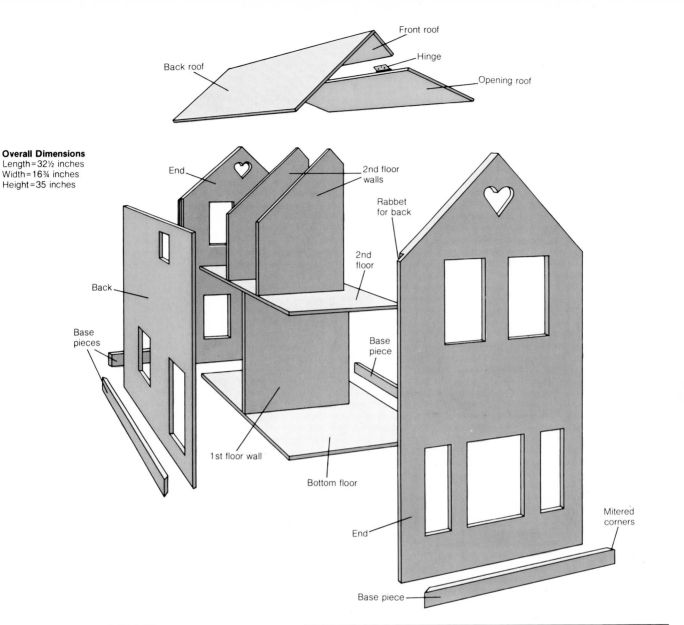

Overall Dimensions
Length = 32½ inches
Width = 16¾ inches
Height = 35 inches

Labels on diagram: Back roof · Front roof · Hinge · Opening roof · End · 2nd floor walls · Rabbet for back · 2nd floor · Back · Base pieces · Base piece · 1st floor wall · Bottom floor · End · Mitered corners · Base piece

CONSTRUCTION

Step 1. Mill all the pieces, mitering the bases at a 45-degree angle.

Step 2. Use the patterns here to mark and cut the gables and windows (see pages 86-87).

Step 3. Cut a rabbet in the ends, ½-inch wide by ¼-inch deep, to accept the back (see page 87).

Step 4. Assemble the house with glue and nails, in the following order: start with the ends, floors, and first-floor wall; add the back, the second-floor walls, and the back and front roofs; then add the base.

Step 5. Hinge the opening roof to the front roof.

Step 6. After removing excess glue and sanding the edges, you can start painting, decorating, and furnishing the house.

LUMBER TO BUY		MILL TO		FOR PROJECT PIECE
Birch plywood (finished both sides)				
1	½" × 4' × 8'	2	½" × 15⅞" × 32½"	Ends
		1	½" × 32½" × 25⅜"	Back
		1	½" × 15⅜" × 32"	Bottom floor
		1	½" × 12" × 32"	Second floor
		1	½" × 14" × 36"	Back roof
		1	½" × 4½" × 36"	Front roof
		1	½" × 9" × 36"	Opening roof
		1	½" × 12" × 12½"	First floor wall
		2	½" × 9" × 18"	Second floor walls
Pine door-stop				
1	½" × 1½" × 10'	2	½" × 1½" × 24"	Base
		2	½" × 1½" × 17"	

Hardware & Miscellaneous
3d finishing nails
1 pair 1½" butt hinges
Glue

TOY CHEST

Here's an attractive, sturdy chest to hide the clutter of toys. It's very simple to build, and good for learning some basic woodworking skills. Most of the brass hardware is decorative, but the adjustable-tension lid supports are indispensable. When adjusted properly these prevent the lid from falling on a child who is reaching into the chest.

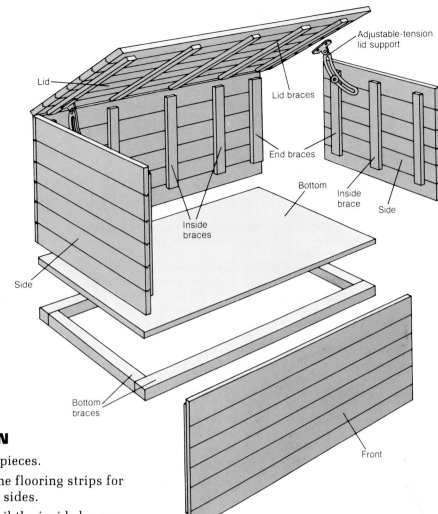

Lid

Adjustable-tension lid support

Lid braces

End braces

Inside braces

Bottom

Inside brace

Side

Side

Bottom braces

Front

CONSTRUCTION

Step 1. Mill all the pieces.

Step 2. Assemble the flooring strips for the front, back, and sides.

Step 3. Glue and nail the inside braces ¾ inch below all the top edges, ¾ inch from the edges of the front and back, and 1½ inches from the side edges. Use a framing square to assure accuracy. Place the remaining braces equally, as shown.

Step 4. Assemble the lid in the same way, attaching the end braces ⅞ inch from the edges and spacing the others evenly.

Step 5. Glue and nail the sides to the front and back by driving 6-penny nails through the sides into the end braces of the front and back. Set the nails (see page 96).

Step 6. Place the bottom braces on the D or blemished side of the plywood flush with the edges, and glue and nail the braces to the bottom.

Step 7. Turn the chest upside down. Glue the outside edges of the bottom braces and set the bottom—good side down—into place against the inside braces. Secure it by driving three or four 6-penny nails through each side into the bottom braces. Set the nails and remove excess glue.

Step 8. Fill the nail holes, and finish the chest and lid as desired.

Step 9. Secure the lid to the chest with the piano hinge, attach and adjust the lid supports, and mount the handles and corners.

LUMBER TO BUY		MILL TO		FOR PROJECT PIECE
Fir T&G flooring (grade A select)				
6	1"× 4"× 14'	12	¾"× 3½"× 40"	Front and back pieces
		12	¾"× 3½"× 20½"	End pieces
		7	¾"× 3½"× 40"	Lid pieces
Fir (grade A or B select)				
3	1"× 2"× 10'	14	¾"× 1¾"× 15¼"	Inside braces
		5	¾"× 1¾"× 20¼"	Lid braces
1	2"× 2"× 10'	2	1¾"× 1¾"× 38½"	Bottom braces
		2	1¾"× 1¾"× 17"	
Fir plywood (AD grade)				
1	½"× 2'× 4'	1	½"× 20"× 38½"	Bottom

Hardware & Miscellaneous	
3d finishing nails	8 brass corners (for chest)
6d finishing nails	4 brass corners (for lid)
40" brass piano hinge	Wood putty
2 brass adjustable-tension lid supports	Glue
2 brass handles	

TEETER TOTTER

This indoor teeter totter is small enough for two-year-olds to mount by themselves, and sturdy enough for Mom and Dad. It won't tip when one child gets off, and can be ridden without a playmate. To make it even safer for small children to use, we suggest rounding over all exposed edges.

CONSTRUCTION

Step 1. Mill all stock to size.

Step 2. Draw the rocker design on paper and transfer it to the wood, using a radius of 76½ inches for the top and 80 inches for the bottom. Use a 1-inch layout grid to draw the end curve, and use the first cut rocker as a model for the second. Round over the top edges.

Step 3. Draw and cut the duck and chicken heads and tails, or use the shapes of your kids' favorite animals. Rout and drill the facial details and round over the exposed edges. Glue the four ½-inch dowel plugs into the eyes.

Step 4. Draw and cut the seat and back patterns as shown in the illustration. Either dado a groove in the rear edge of the seats, or cut the rear edge of the seats and the bottom edge of the backs at a 60-degree angle. Round over the exposed edges.

Step 5. Cut the bottom and side angles of the legs at 75 and 105 degrees, respectively. Round over the top outside corner.

Step 6. Follow the rocker pattern and cut a curve on one end of each side piece. Cut the other end at a 5-degree angle.

Step 7. After measuring carefully to leave room for the seats and backs, glue and screw the animal heads and tails and the spacer block between the sides. Countersink the screws and glue dowel caps over them.

Step 8. Glue and screw the legs to the sides. Set the end legs perpendicular to the sides and 7½ inches from the ends; the middle legs parallel to and directly over the center joint of the sides. All legs should be exactly 1 inch from the top of the sides.

Step 9. Glue and screw the base pieces to the bottoms of the legs, making sure the legs are centered exactly.

Step 10. Glue and screw the rockers to the base pieces. The middle base piece should be centered in the middle of the rockers about ½ inch below the top edge. The end base-pieces may be attached to the rockers slightly higher or lower than the middle one, but both should be equal. Countersink and cap all the screws.

Step 11. Glue and nail the seats and backs in place, using 6-penny finishing nails.

Step 12. Center and glue the dowels through the holes in the animal heads, and insert a finishing nail into each dowel through the back of the head.

Step 13. Clean off excess glue and sand carefully. Finish as desired.

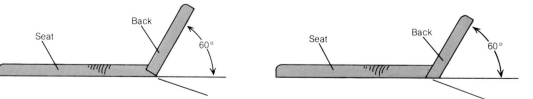

Rabbet at a 60-degree angle or...　　　　Cut rear edge of seat and bottom edge of back at a 60-degree angle.

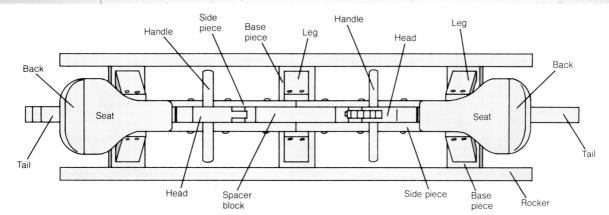

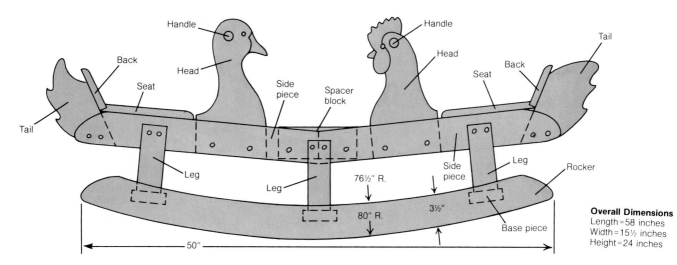

Overall Dimensions
Length = 58 inches
Width = 15½ inches
Height = 24 inches

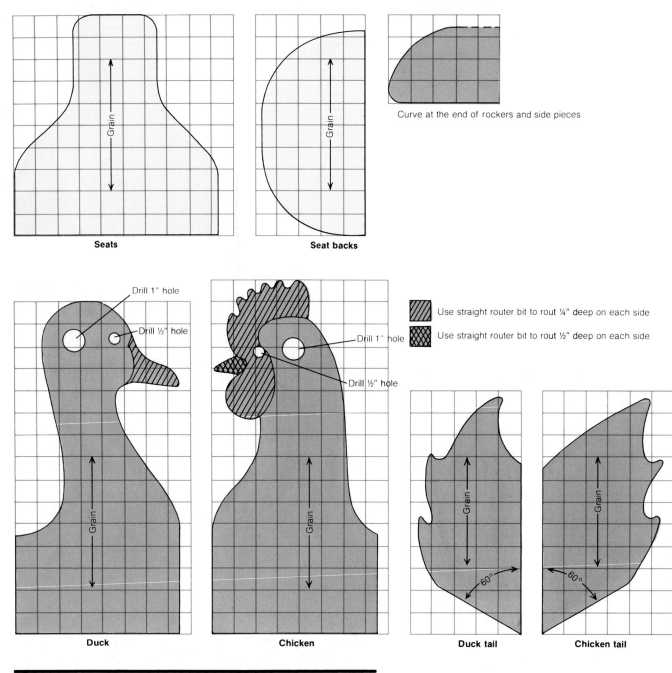

Seats

Seat backs

Curve at the end of rockers and side pieces

Drill 1" hole

Drill ½" hole

Duck

Drill 1" hole

Drill ½" hole

Chicken

Use straight router bit to rout ¼" deep on each side

Use straight router bit to rout ½" deep on each side

Duck tail

60°

Chicken tail

60°

LUMBER TO BUY			MILL TO		FOR PROJECT PIECE
Fir (grade A select)					
3	2"× 8"× 6'		2	1½"× 7¼"× 51"	Rockers
			2	1½"× 7¼"× 15"	Heads
			2	1½"× 7¼"× 10"	Tails
1	1"× 10"× 4'		2	¾"× 9¼"× 10"	Seats
			2	¾"× 9¼"× 8"	Backs
1	2"× 4"× 10'		3	1½"× 3½"× 12"	Bases
			1	1½"× 3½"× 8"	Spacer
			6	1½"× 3"× 10"	Legs
1	1"× 4"× 10'		4	¾"× 3½"× 26"	Sides
Maple or birch dowel					
1	1" dia.× 2'		2	1" dia.× 10"	Handles

Hardware & Miscellaneous
56 ⅜" dowel caps
4 ½" dowel caps
56 2½" #8 flat-head wood screws
6 6d finishing nails
Glue

CHILD'S BED

This could be a lovely, first "real bed" for your child—or a fine bed for anyone. Its beauty is simplicity and grace, and it retains its lines at any scale. We built ours for a crib mattress, which will fit most children to age eight. You can build a twin bed the same way, using the second set of dimensions. For a larger mattress, add extra bracing beneath the plywood.

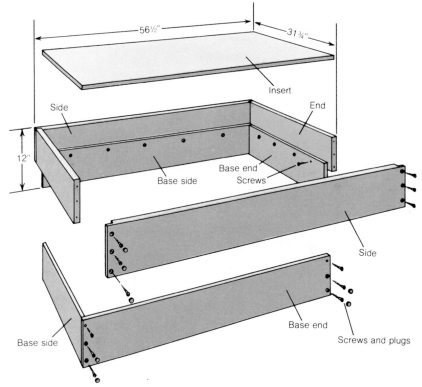

CONSTRUCTION

Step 1. Mill the lumber to size.

Step 2. Cut rabbets 1-inch deep by 1¾ inches wide in both ends of each bed side (see page 87).

Step 3. Drill three ⅛-inch pilot holes through each corner joint of the bed ends, and use ¾-inch counterbores for the dowel plugs in the sides (see page 89).

Step 4. Assemble the bed sides and ends with glue and #12 screws, and glue in the dowel plugs.

Step 5. For the base, drill three 3⁄32-inch pilot holes through each corner joint, and counterbore the two lowest ones with a ⅜-inch bit for the dowel plugs.

Step 6. Assemble the base sides and ends with glue and 2-inch #10 screws, then glue in the dowel plugs.

Step 7. When the glue is dry, cut the dowel plugs flush and sand both sections.

Step 8. Set the bed frame over the base, using blocks to hold it 4½ inches above the floor. Screw the base to the frame from the inside with the 1½-inch #10 screws, after drilling 3⁄32-inch pilot holes.

Step 9. Finish the wood as desired.

Step 10. Sand the top of the plywood insert and drop it in place.

LUMBER TO BUY		MILL TO		PROJECT PIECE
Crib-size bed				
Oak (FAS grade)				
2	2"× 8"× 8'	2	1¾"× 7½"× 56"	Bed sides
		2	1¾"× 7½"× 30¼"	Bed ends
2	1"× 8"× 8'	2	¾"× 7½"× 53"	Base sides
		2	¾"× 7½"× 26¾"	Base ends
Fir plywood				
1	¾"× 3'× 5'	1	¾"× 28¼"× 53"	Insert
Twin-size bed				
3	2"× 8"× 8'	2	1¾"× 7½"× 79½"	Bed sides
		2	1¾"× 7½"× 41"	Bed ends
2	1"× 8"× 8'	2	¾"× 7½"× 76"	Base sides
1	1"× 8"× 6'	2	¾"× 7½"× 37½"	Base ends
Fir plywood				
1	¾"× 4'× 8'	1	¾"× 39"× 76"	Insert
Dowel (for either size)				
1	¾" dia.× 1'	12	¾" pieces	Dowel plugs
1	⅜" dia.× 1'	12	½" pieces	

Hardware & Miscellaneous	
12 3"× #12 flat-head wood screws	16 1½"× #10 flat-head wood screws
12 2"× #10 flat-head wood screws	Glue

ROCKING HORSE

This will delight even a 90-year-old child. It's a whimsical sculpture for any room in the house, and as much fun to build as to play with. We used a small chain saw, a router, an electric drill with a drum-rasp and disc-sanding attachments, a surform plane, and wood-sculpting knives and chisels. A strong partner will help for assembly.

CONSTRUCTION

Step 1. Mill all the lumber.

Step 2. Check the illustrations for measurements and angles, then notch the sides of the body to accept the legs, as well as the front end of the body, so it will be flush with the front of the legs.

Step 3. Follow the side- and front-view illustrations to cut notches in the bottom of each leg—1-inch deep by 4½ inches, at the same angle used to notch the body—so they can be set on the rockers. Then cut each leg into its rough shape with a band, reciprocating, or chain saw.

Step 4. To attach the legs, use a forstner bit to drill four 1-inch by 1-inch holes in each leg to countersink the screws. Then drill a ¼-inch pilot hole 6 inches deep through the center of each counterbore into the body, and insert the lag screws and washers with a socket wrench.

Step 5. Cut a 45-degree angle in the upper end of the neck, and in the bottom end cut a 97-degree notch at a 45-degree angle (see illustration).

Step 6. Cut the back end of the head at a 40-degree angle.

Step 7. Assemble the head and neck by putting two countersunk 6-inch lag screws and washers through the neck and one through the head.

Step 8. Rough cut the head and neck using a band, reciprocating, or chain saw.

Step 9. Attach the head and neck assembly to the body with six countersunk 6-inch lag screws and washers.

Step 10. Glue dowel plugs into all the screw holes and cut them flush with the surface after they've dried.

Step 11. Sculpt the horse as you wish.

Step 12. Draw the rocker on the 4 by 12 lumber. The radius of the top curve is 90 inches, the bottom 95 inches.

Step 13. Mill the rockers with a band or reciprocating saw, and round over the top edges (see page 88).

Step 14. Screw the horse to the rockers with countersunk 4½-inch lag screws and washers after sliding the horse back and forth until it balances on the rockers. At rest, both ends of the rockers should be equidistant from the floor.

Step 15. Clean, sand, and finish.

Step 16. Affix the eyes, mane, and tail.

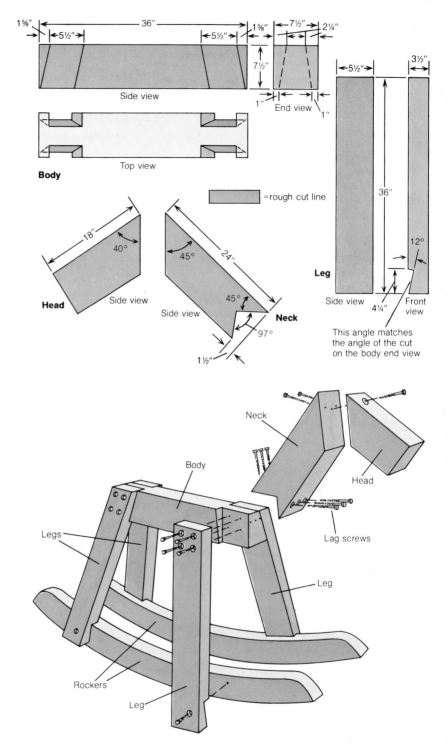

LUMBER TO BUY		MILL TO		FOR PROJECT PIECE
Fir (No. 1 grade select)				
1	8"× 8"× 8'	1	7½"× 7½"× 36"	Body
		1	7½"× 7½"× 24"	Neck
		1	7½"× 7½"× 18"	Head
1	4"× 6"× 12"	4	3½"× 3½"× 36"	Legs
1	4"× 12"× 12'	2	3½"× 11¼"× 72"	Rockers
Dowel				
1	1" dia.× 3'	28	1" dia.× 1"	Plugs

Hardware & Miscellaneous	
25 ⅜" dia.× 6" lag screws; washers	2 eyes (horse eyes from a taxidermist, glass marbles, or wooden dowels)
4 ⅜" dia.× 4½" lag screws; washers	
	Mane and tail (horse hair, or unbraided rope or yarn)

ABOUT LUMBER

Lumber sizes

The sawmills cut lumber into standard sizes, from 1 to 8 or more inches thick and 4 to 12 or more inches wide. This rough lumber is then "dressed" or "surfaced" with planing machines that remove ⅛ inch or more from the sides and edges.

You can't be sure of a board's exact size when you buy it; the planing machines don't always remove the same amount, and humiditity will also affect the size of the lumber. However, when you you buy lumber it is still known by its nominal or rough size.

The standard thicknesses of surfaced softwoods and hardwoods also differ somewhat, as shown on the chart.

Buying softwoods

Softwood lumber—pine, fir, cedar, redwood, etc.—is usually available in the standard thicknesses and widths shown on the chart, and in lengths of 6 feet to 20 feet in 2-foot increments.

Buying hardwoods

Hardwood is usually available in a greater variety of thicknesses, and comes in random widths and lengths. Often the edges retain the curves of the original tree. When buying hardwood, calculate ahead of time the sizes and number of pieces you'll need, and take that list to the lumberyard so you'll get enough of the proper lengths. Also, as hardwood boards are often split near the ends, purchase pieces about 1 foot longer than you actually need.

Most lumberyards will straighten the edges and mill your lumber to the sizes you'll need. If you'd like to economize and do it yourself, build a jig or two as shown in the drawings on page 87.

Lumber grades

There are three basic classifications of softwood: select, common, and structural. Select is further divided into grades A, B, C, and D, with D representing the lowest quality. Grade A select, sometimes called "clear" because it has practically no blemishes, and grade B, which has only a few, are both suitable for clear or natural finishes. Grades C and D have increasingly more knots and larger blemishes, but they are tight and smooth and can be covered by paint.

For these projects you will need the best grades of hardwood, which are designated "firsts" and "seconds"; usually these are combined and referred to as FAS grade (firsts and seconds). Other grades suitable for our projects, in descending order, are select, #1 common, and #2 common.

Plywood

Plywood is made of several layers or plies of wood, which are glued together with the grains of adjacent layers arranged at right angles. Plywood thus has equal strength in both directions and is less likely than regular lumber to warp, split, or check.

Plywood is avaiiable with soft or hardwood faces, as described below. Many beautiful hardwoods, which usually come in narrow widths, are now available as veneered plywoods. You can get the veneer on one or both sides, and these panels are referred to as hardwood plywood even though only the face ply is hardwood. This is used in most commercially manufactured furniture, especially for large flat visible areas. The backs and drawer bottoms of furniture usually are made of softwood plywood.

Softwood plywood

Common plywood is almost always Douglas fir, which comes in grades A, B, C, and D and is designated either interior or exterior. Exterior plywood is bonded with waterproof glue and will withstand moisture. Each side of a sheet of plywood is graded separately. If both sides will be visible you'll want A-A or A-B grade; if only one side will be seen you can get grade A-D. Douglas fir plywood is usually available in 4-foot by 8-foot panels in thicknesses of ¼, ⅜, ½, ⅝, and ¾ inch.

Hardwood plywood

We used the premium and good grades for natural-finish projects, and the sound grade for painted projects. The premium grade has select, smoothly cut veneers with carefully matched grain and color. The good grade is similar, but the grain isn't matched as carefully. Sound grade is not matched for grain or color, but it is smooth and has no open defects.

Hardwood plywood is made in these thicknesses: ⅛, $\frac{3}{16}$, ¼, $\frac{5}{16}$, ⅜, ½, ⅝ and ¾ inch. Most domestic hardwood plywood comes in 4-foot by 8-foot panels, although usually dealers will cut and sell you a smaller sheet.

Some of the finest hardwood plywood is made abroad and comes in sizes other than 4 by 8 feet. The Finn or Baltic birch we used for the doll house, for example, is available only in 5-foot by 5-foot panels. It is finished on both sides and has no voids in the middle.

Hardboard and particle board

These are manufactured from wood fibers and chips that are combined with adhesives and pressed to form panels. In our projects we've used particle board for tops that will be covered with plastic laminate, and hardboard for the drawing surface of the easel. Hardboard can also be used for drawer bottoms, but it doesn't look as nice as a wood veneer.

Dowels

Dowels are used for two purposes in our projects: as important structural features (in the dish rack, magazine rack, and one of the trivets), or as invisible reinforcements for joints. Most lumberyards and many hardware stores have both.

Smooth dowels usually are made of either maple or birch and come in diameters of ⅛, ¼, ⅜, ½, ⅝, ¾, ⅞, and 1 inch. They are commonly sold in either 3- or 4-foot lengths.

The joinery, or grooved, dowels are generally available in diameters of ¼, ⅜, and ½ inch, and in lengths from 1 to 3 inches. The longitudinal or spiral grooves allow the glue to flow freely and let air escape when the joint is clamped. They usually have chamfered ends to make insertion easier.

PLASTIC LAMINATE

Working table, counter, and desk tops are often made of plastic laminate, also known by their trade names: Formica, Micarta, Nevamar, Panelyte, Texolite, and others. The laminates for this purpose are ¹⁄₁₆-inch thick and are found in widths of 24, 30, 48, and 60 inches. Common lengths are 60, 72, 84, 96, and 120 inches. See page 92 for cutting instructions.

ADHESIVES

Wood glue

Where glue is listed we mean either polyvinyl resin (white) glue or aliphatic resin (ivory) glue. The latter is stronger. It can be used in temperatures as low as 50 degrees F., and is more resistant to heat. Both set in an hour or less at room temperature.

Contact cement

A ready-mixed neoprene rubber in liquid form is ideal for bonding plastic laminates to plywood or particle board. Apply the cement to both surfaces with a brush or paint roller, and let it dry until the gloss is gone. The laminate bonds to the wood instantly on contact, so be sure they are aligned properly before they touch each other.

Cork paste adhesive

Because cork is fragile, crumbly, and porous, it is best to use special cork paste adhesive or linoleum paste for projects such as the bulletin board. These are sticky enough to hold the cork as soon as you place it, but will allow you to move it around for proper alignment.

MILLING

For many of the techniques in this section we are assuming you have some power equipment —at least an electric drill and either a radial arm or a table saw. Of course, all of the operations done with this equipment can be done with hand tools— before about 1930 they all were —but most of the tools and much of the skill to use them are hard to come by these days.

Ripping and cutting

Check your lumber carefully so you know the thickness and width of all the stock. If the variance in the actual size of the wood will make a difference in the project's "mill to" dimensions, note it and make changes accordingly.

A good rule-of-thumb for milling is "rip to width, then cut to length." That is, first cut the stock to its required width, or rip smaller widths from the stock. If you have a very sharp saw blade—preferably a combination planing blade—the cuts will be smooth enough to use without additional planing.

As mentioned in "buying hardwoods," the lengths and widths

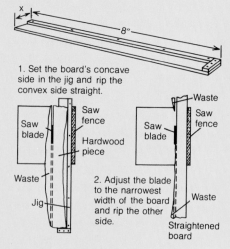

1. Set the board's concave side in the jig and rip the convex side straight.

2. Adjust the blade to the narrowest width of the board and rip the other side.

are often random and ragged. To straighten this kind of board, build a jig or two of ¼-inch plywood and some 1 by 2 lumber as shown in the drawings.

Note carefully if any of the projects call for an angle cut going with the direction of the grain. (The cedar chest lid slats require this cut.) Set your saw for the angle indicated and mind which side of the board you need to have up, to make the angles go the right way.

When all the stock is ripped to the widths needed, set your saw for cross-cutting and cut all the lengths.

Miter joints

If some boards need to be cut at angles, like miter joints, first measure the length and mark it on all the boards to be cut at the same angle. Then set the saw for the angle you need and cut the boards. The lengths given in the "mill to" column are to the longest points on angle-cut boards.

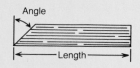

Drawer fronts

There are at least two ways to cut drawer fronts out of their surrounding edging. (This is required in the corner desk project.) Our preferred method, with a table saw, is to set the saw fence for either the width of the drawer front or the rail above it. Lower the board onto the saw and cut carefully just to the edge of the drawer front. Then cross-cut the ends of the drawer fronts —again, just to the edge. Finish the cuts with a handsaw.

Another way, with a saber saw, is to drill contiguous holes, the thickness of the blade, in the center of the top line of the drawer front—as many as you need to insert the saber saw blade. Insert the blade in the slot and saw to each corner. Repeat the process for the ends.

OTHER SAW OPERATIONS

A radial arm, table, or portable circular saw, in addition to ripping and cutting, can be used to make rabbets, dadoes, and grooves with its single blade. By adding dado blades and a molding head with a variety of cutter sets you can also do any number of shaping, joining, and planing operations. The operations used in this book are explained below.

Dadoing

Dadoes or grooves of any width can be made with a single saw blade set to cut only part way through the board. For each groove, draw the shape on the end or edge of the board and set the blade to the proper depth. Make the two outside cuts to the width you want, and then make as many passes as needed to clean out the middle.

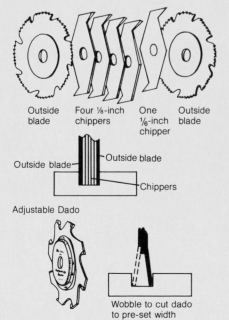

Outside blade — Four ⅛-inch chippers — One ⅛-inch chipper — Outside blade

Outside blade — Outside blade — Chippers

Adjustable Dado

Wobble to cut dado to pre-set width

Power saws have two kinds of dado attachments. One is a set of matched blades, which you add or subtract to get the desired groove width. The other is a single blade that has an adjustable wobble. Except for the blade changing, the saw set-up is the same as it is for regular ripping or cutting. To be safe, always use a guard and make your cuts slowly; and always read and understand the instructions that come with the attachment.

The typical dado set has seven blades: two ⅛-inch-thick outside cutters; four ⅛-inch-thick chippers; and one ¹⁄₁₆-inch-thick chipper. Use one outside blade for a ⅛-inch groove; two outside blades to cut a ¼-inch groove; and larger widths in ¹⁄₁₆-inch increments by adding the chippers between the outside blades. Additional adjustments of width can be made by adding paper washers (shims) between the blades and the chippers.

The adjustable dado blade is usually carbide tipped and has a self-contained wobbler unit that can be set to let the blade oscillate from side to side at a predetermined amount as the blade revolves. The typical blade cuts a kerf from ³⁄₁₆ inch up to ¹³⁄₁₆ inch. The kerfs are adjusted by the rotation of a dial calibrated in ¹⁄₁₆-inch increments. The adjustment is continuous, not stepped, allowing variations of less than ¹⁄₁₆ inch. The bottom of these cuts may be slightly bowed.

Rabbeting

Two cuts are needed to make a rabbet: the first is made from going in from the side, horizontally, and the second is made by going down from the top. (See the equipment manual for the horizontal set-up.) The vertical set-up is the same as it would be for ripping or cutting.

For each rabbet, draw the shape on the end of the board and make your set-ups accordingly. Plan your second cut to

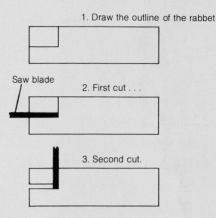

1. Draw the outline of the rabbet

Saw blade   2. First cut . . .

3. Second cut.

meet the first, as shown in the drawing.

To cut rabbets in a single operation, use either of the dado attachments or the molding head with a planer blade (see shaping and planing). Just set the blades to cut the edge of the board.

Lap joints

The power saw with a dado attachment can be used to cut any of the notches needed for lap joints. If the notch is wider than the ¹³⁄₁₆-inch maximum, multiple passes are necessary. Make the two outside passes first and then clean out the middle of the notch.

Shaping and planing

Molding heads, like those shown, make your radial arm saw into an incredibly versatile shaper. They can do surface molding and planing as well as edge shaping.

For planing and jointing—that is, smoothing an edge for gluing— set the straight molding head in

Some common molding cutter blades

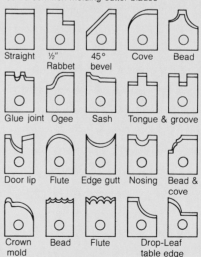

Straight — ½" Rabbet — 45° bevel — Cove — Bead

Glue joint — Ogee — Sash — Tongue & groove

Door lip — Flute — Edge gutt — Nosing — Bead & cove

Crown mold — Bead — Flute — Drop-Leaf table edge

a horizontal position. All edge operations are done with a ripping set-up, with the molding head positioned behind the fence. A molding head guard *must* be used for all edge shaping.

By using a vertical cross-cutting set-up and straight cutters, you can plane the surfaces of flat pieces like the cutting boards. Set the cutters to remove about $\frac{1}{16}$ inch of surface, move the work along the fence, and pull and push the saw across it (see drawing).

Chamfering
Either the dado blades or the molding head with planing blades can be used to chamfer the edge of a board. Set the saw for a ripping operation with the molding head or blades behind the fence. Position the blade at the angle you want, so when the board is moved along the fence the corner is removed to the depth you want.

To start and stop a chamfer before the end of a board, as we did on the sides of the bed table, first mark the places where you want the chamfer to start and stop. Then lay the board you want chamfered on the saw table, away from the fence, and positioned so the mark is opposite the cutter. Push the board into the blade, slide it along the fence until you reach the second mark, and pull it away from the fence again.

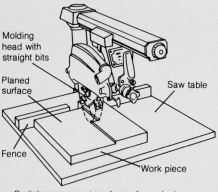

Radial arm saw set-up for surface planing

Tapering
To taper the legs of the kitchen island or any other piece of lumber, either buy an adjustable ta-

pering jig or make one like those shown in the drawings. For the kitchen island we recommend tapering only the adjacent exterior sides of each leg, so you only need to make the "one-side" jig or set one angle on the adjustable jig. Set the saw for ripping and slide the jig along the fence as the blade cuts the taper. Rotate the leg one quarter and repeat the process.

For a symmetrical taper (equal on all four sides of a leg) you'll need the "two-side" jig or two different openings on the adjustable jig. First do two adjoining sides with the first jig set-up, as described above, and then do the remaining two sides with the second jig setting.

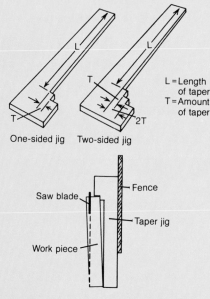

One-sided jig   Two-sided jig

L = Length of taper
T = Amount of taper

ROUTER
The portable electric router is very versatile and performs many functions. We will discuss only those that apply to our projects.

Dadoing
Use one of several straight-face bits, which come in sizes from $\frac{1}{8}$ inch to $\frac{3}{4}$ inch for a $\frac{1}{4}$-inch chuck. Set the depth you want to cut and use a guide-fence attachment or a board clamped to the work as a guide (see drawings).

For a wider groove you can make one cut, then adjust the guide and make a second pass, and continue the process until

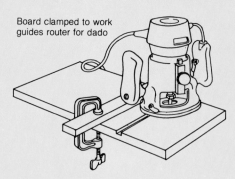

Board clamped to work guides router for dado

the groove is as wide as you need it. Another method is to clamp two boards to the work, run the router against each in turn, and then move it freely between the two boards to clean out the center of the groove.

Rabbeting
Use either a rabbet bit with a pilot tip set to the proper depth or, for a wider rabbet, set up an edge guide for the inside edge, as shown for dadoes, and let the router run off the edge on the outside.

Shaping and rounding over
Edge shaping with a round-over, beading, chamfer, cove, Roman ogee, or any other bit with a pilot tip, is done by running the router along the edge of the work. Just be sure that the edge is smooth and true—the bit will reproduce any irregularities exactly.

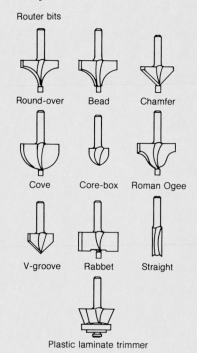

Router bits

Round-over   Bead   Chamfer

Cove   Core-box   Roman Ogee

V-groove   Rabbet   Straight

Plastic laminate trimmer

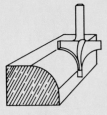 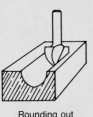

Rounding over   Rounding out

Rounding out

A core-box bit is used for rounding out, and you will need either a guide-fence attachment or a board clamped to the work to guide the router. If you want the groove to stop before it reaches the end of the work, switch the router on before lowering it vertically onto the surface where you want the groove to start; make the cut to the point where you want it to end, and lift the router clear before switching it off.

Chamfering

You can use a chamfer bit with a pilot tip or a v-groove bit. The latter is good to use if you want to take off less than the bit is designed for, in which case you would clamp a board to the work in the proper position and use it as a guide.

Cutting and edging plastic laminate.

See page 92 for the methods used.

DRILLING

All operations described here can be performed with either an electric drill or a hand or breast drill. However, because a ¼-inch or ⅜-inch electric drill is so useful and inexpensive, we recommend that you get one.

Dowel joints

Dowel holes can be drilled with either a twist drill or a dowel bit, which has spurs and a center point to keep it from following the grain and wandering off center.

To make well-aligned dowel joints follow the steps outlined here.

Step 1. Hold the pieces of wood together, as they will butt, and mark the dowel position on the edge.
Step 2. Set a dowel jig to position the dowels in the center of the wood.
Step 3. Align the pencil mark with the center mark on the jig and clamp the jig to the work. Insert the drill bit into the guide and drill to the required depth. Repeat the process for each hole.

Dowel pins can also be used to position dowel holes. These are double-pointed pins that look like two thumbtacks glued together. Follow these steps.
Step 1. Press a pin into each marked center.
Step 2. Align the second half of the joint, onto the pins and press it firmly onto the points.
Step 3. Remove the pins and drill the holes.

When the holes are drilled correctly, put glue into the holes, insert the dowels, and clamp the work.

Drilling to depth

You can buy a depth gauge that attaches to your drill, or wrap a piece of masking or electrician's tape around the bit where you want to stop drilling.

Countersinking screws

Three boring operations are necessary to countersink a screw properly. First clamp or hold the pieces together in proper alignment. Then drill the pilot hole, shank hole, and countersink in that order, using bits the proper size for the screws you are using. When the holes are drilled for all the screws, remove the clamps, apply the glue, and drive the screws into place.

To counterbore a screw hole you'll also need to bore three holes: the pilot hole, the shank hole, and the counterbore. Special combination bits will perform all three operations in one step. There are also plug-cutter bits that match the sizes of the drill-and-counter-bore bits,

which enable you to cut matching or contrasting plugs to cover the screws.

JOINTS

Your choice of joints will be based on several factors: How easily you can make the joint using the tools you have; the strength and rigidity required; and how the joint will look on the finished project. Usually, the easiest joint you can make for the job is the one you should use.

We used the simplest joints to give the look and the strength we wanted, and these are shown and described below. Many more variations exist.

Butt joints

These are obviously the easiest joints to make. They are also the weakest unless reinforced. Cut the pieces to the lengths needed to meet each other and then hold them together with glue and nails, screws, or dowels as you wish.

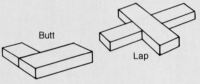

Butt   Lap

Rabbet joints

These are used for most drawer construction, for attaching the back panel to most cabinets and cases, and for places where end grain or grooves need to be hidden. They provide more strength than a butt joint because there is more surface to glue.

For neatness, the rabbet should be cut precisely to fit the width and thickness of the joining piece. It can be cut with a circular saw or a router, shaper, or jointer.

On any freestanding cabinet the rabbet for the back panel should be cut exactly deep enough to hold the back flush with the sides and top. On built-ins that will be attached to a wall, cut the rabbet ¼ inch to ¾ inch deeper than the thickness of the back. This leaves plenty of material to trim when you fit the project to an uneven wall.

When marking the sizes of pieces to be joined with a rabbet, allow for the extra length of the piece that fits into the joint.

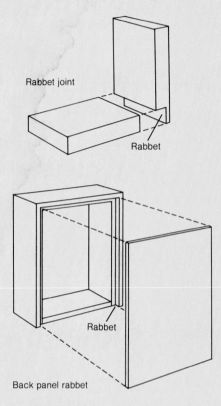

Rabbet joint

Rabbet

Rabbet

Back panel rabbet

Dado/groove joints

This kind of joint is usually used where a supporting edge is needed for added strength, or where one of the members is too thin or difficult to attach with nails, screws, dowels, or other reinforcements.

The depth of a dado should never be more than half the thickness of the piece it is cut into. Be sure to add the depth of the dado to the length of the piece that goes into it.

Lap joints

For these, an equal section is cut from both pieces to be joined so they fit together flush. The lap joints we show are those used for our projects. They can be cut with multiple passes of a saw blade, or with a dado attachment on a saw or a router.

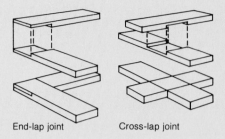

End-lap joint   Cross-lap joint

Miter joints

Miter joints are used most commonly to connect the complex edges of shaped lumber or moldings (as in picture frames), and to conceal the end grain of pieces to be joined. They are relatively weak unless reinforced with nails, screws, or other fasteners.

Mortise and tenon

Many kinds of mortise and tenon joints are used in furniture construction to hold legs, rails, and skirts together, although dowel- or screw-reinforced butt joints are just as strong and durable. We used mortise and tenon joints on the sawbuck table and the firewood tower because they add to the appearance of those projects.

Unless you have a special mortise-cutting attachment for a drill press, the mortise is best made by drilling many holes around the edges and then cutting the sides smooth and precise with a chisel. Cut the mortise too small rather than too large, as you can always enlarge it with a rasp.

Edge joints

Edge joints are used to make larger boards from smaller ones, as for a plank tabletop, the round supports in the lid of the cedar chest, or when gluing together many small pieces to make a cutting board or chopping block. Often there is enough gluing surface that added reinforcement isn't necessary. However, to reinforce the joints you can dowel the boards together or use tongue-and-groove joints (as on the oak parson's table).

When using dowels, space them about 6 to 8 inches apart

and alternate them from board to board as shown in the drawing. When gluing pieces for a rustic tabletop, like the sawbuck table, you might consider chamfering a v-groove in the edges of each board where they meet.

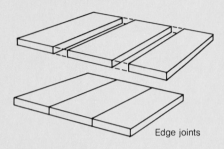

Edge joints

Gluing and clamping

The strongest glue joints are made on surfaces that are smooth and blemish-free, with a layer of glue covering the surfaces competely and evenly. If you are gluing end grain, first seal the end grain with a slightly diluted glue mixture before applying the rest of the glue.

The application of pressure to a glue joint forces out air bubbles and forces the glue into a thin film between tightly fitting wood surfaces. When nails or screws are not being used, as with edge or dowel joints, clamps should be used to apply the pressure and to keep the parts properly aligned until the glue sets.

SHELVES

There is more than one way to install shelves, and you should use the method that is easiest for you.

Fixed shelves

Butt joint. Where cabinet shelves extend from one side to another, the shelves can be glued and nailed from the outside.
Reinforced butt joint. When you can't nail into the end of the shelf from the outside, the shelf can be glued to the side and held in place with a wooden cleat that is glued and nailed or screwed to the side. A face frame on the cabinet will help conceal the cleats, and so will quarter-round molding.

Dado joint. A dado adds a more professional, finished look to your work, and a great deal of strength and rigidity.

Adjustable shelves

Notch and cleat. Prior to all the metal and plastic pins, cleats, and brackets, many cabinet shelves were made adjustable with this all-wood method (illustrated in the glossary). In each of the four corners of the cabinet, position a ½-inch-thick by 1-inch-wide strip that is notched every inch. A ½-inch by ¾-inch cleat fits into these notches to hold the shelf. The shelves must have cutouts at each corner to fit around the notched strips.

Dowel pins. Drill a series of ¼-inch holes in the side of the cabinet, an inch or two from the front and back edges of the shelf. Insert a short length of ¼-inch dowel in the holes at the height you want the shelf and rest the shelf on the dowels.

Plastic or metal clips. Instead of dowel pins, use commercially manufactured plastic or metal clips to hold the shelf.

Pilasters and clips. These perforated metal pilasters can be mounted either on the surface or flush with the cabinet sides (as illustrated in the glossary). If surface-mounted, the shelves must be cut shorter than the cabinet width or notched to accommodate the pilasters. If flush-mounted, you must cut a groove in the side of the cabinet before assembly.

Doors

There are three basic kinds of hinged doors for cabinets and chests: overlap, flush, and lip. The flush doors in our projects can be made into lip doors by adding ¾ inch to the overall dimensions of the doors and shaping the edges as shown in the drawing. A special cutter for this edge will fit a molding head attachment (see page 87). For double doors, don't shape the edges where the doors meet. The additional ¾ inch is for both doors together.

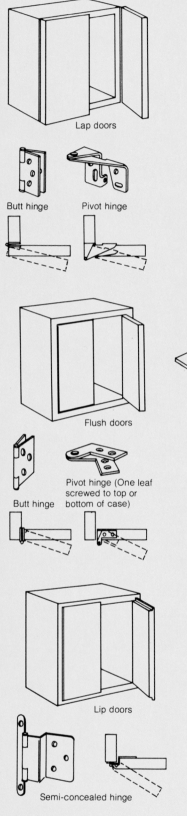

Lap doors

Butt hinge   Pivot hinge

Flush doors

Butt hinge   Pivot hinge (One leaf screwed to top or bottom of case)

Lip doors

Semi-concealed hinge

DRAWERS

A drawer is just a box made of 5 basic pieces: a front, a back, two sides, and a bottom. The construction can be done simply, with butt joints, or with multiple dovetail or many kinds of rabbet or dado joints.

Our drawers were made by simply joining the sides to the fronts with a dado joint, and the backs to the sides with a butt joint. We slid the bottom into a dado in the sides and front and nailed it to the back, which was ripped flush with the top of the dado.

By gluing and nailing or clamping these joints until dry, the drawer will be strong enough to withstand rough usage.

The three basic types of drawers are flush, overlap, and lip, and the type one chooses is usually a

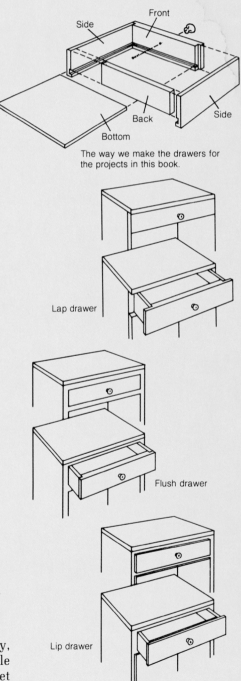

Front
Side
Side
Back
Bottom

The way we make the drawers for the projects in this book.

Lap drawer

Flush drawer

Lip drawer

function of the overall design. Drawer construction is basically similar, regardless of type. Although all drawers should be fitted and built carefully, the lip type allows for some error, as the lip overlaps the face and will cover a small gap. Flush and overlap drawers must fit perfectly or they look sloppy.

Our construction steps are as follows:

Step 1. Measure the opening and inside depth where the drawer will go to determine its outside dimensions.

Step 2. Transfer these dimensions to the lumber, and mill all the pieces.

Step 3. Cut all the dadoes, rabbets, etc., including those across the front, back, and sides if the drawer has partitions.

Step 4. Assemble the front and back to the sides with glue and nails or clamps.

Step 5. Slide the bottom into place and hold it with a couple of nails into the back. (If you dado the back instead of ripping it, the bottom must be put in when you assemble the other pieces.)

Drawer supports and guides

Drawer supports are determined by the construction of the furniture. If a project has a solid bottom, a dust panel, or a frame that is part of the basic construction, this will serve to support the drawers. (This is the case with our sandwich desk, the modular unit basic chest with one drawer over doors, and the kitchen island.) Other projects, like the modular unit chest with several drawers, have a groove in the side of each drawer that slides on a rail attached to the side of the chest.

Several kinds of metal and plastic drawer tracks, slides, and other hardware are available to make installation easier and to make the drawers slide smoother. We used metal drawer slides with plastic rollers for the roll-out drawers. If you use any of these,

carefully choose them and read the directions before you start your project. Some require special clearances, and some require extra cross-members or furring to support brackets or rollers.

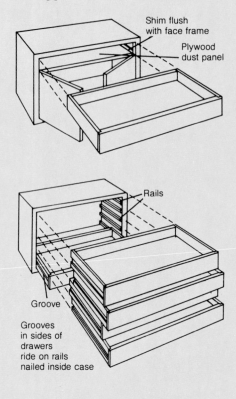

Shim flush with face frame
Plywood dust panel

Rails
Groove
Grooves in sides of drawers ride on rails nailed inside case

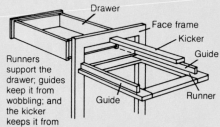

Drawer
Face frame
Kicker
Guide
Runners support the drawer; guides keep it from wobbling; and the kicker keeps it from tipping forward when it's pulled out.
Guide
Runner

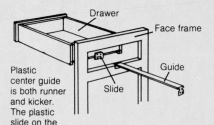

Drawer
Face frame
Plastic center guide is both runner and kicker. The plastic slide on the back of the drawer holds onto the guide.
Guide
Slide

Drawer
Face frame
Metal roller guides
Metal roller drawer guides need extra space between the drawer and face frame and wood shims to hold them flush with the edge of the face frame.
Shim
Shim

PLASTIC LAMINATE

As all of our plastic laminate tops are straight-sided with no concave cuts, the cutting is very easy. One cutting method is to scribe a line on the face side of the laminate with a mat or linoleum knife, or with an awl or special tool made for this purpose. Snap off the excess laminate by laying a straightedge along the scored line and pulling the laminate up. Read the steps below before cutting the laminate for our projects.

You can also use a plywood or special panel saw, or a saber or jig saw with the proper blade. Whatever you use, the blade must be sharp. For curves of any kind you will have to use a saw.

Here are the steps for cutting and applying the plastic laminate to a plywood or particle-board top.

Step 1. Cut the plastic laminate so that it overhangs the wood top ⅛ to ¼ inch on all sides.

Step 2. Paint a generous coat of contact cement on the back of the plastic and the top of the wood with a brush or paint roller.

Step 3. When the cement is no longer glossy, lay large sheets of butcher paper or newspaper on top of the cemented wood. (It won't stick if you've let the cement dry enough.) Leave about ½ inch of cement exposed along one edge.

Step 4. Lay the plastic on top of the paper to align it exactly where you want it before you let it touch the small strip of exposed cement. When the plastic is aligned press it against the exposed strip of cement.

Step 5. Slightly raise the other side from the paper and slide the paper out. Then press the plastic against the wood and it will be bonded permanently.

Step 6. You can use a router with a special plastic laminate trimming bit to cut the plastic flush with the edge. If you don't have a router, trim the laminate with a block plane and touch up the edge with a flat metal file using downward strokes.

Step 7. Apply the side edging flush with the top surface of the plastic.

FINISHING

The kind and quality of finish will contribute greatly to a project's beauty and utility. We will touch only briefly on some of the steps and a few of the easiest and most common techniques. Whatever finish you use, the first step is very important, and is always the same.

Clean-up and smoothing

For many projects we've included some cleaning and sanding in the step-by-step instructions before final assembly. For most other projects pre-sanding would also be good, as it is easier to do and you can follow the grain of the wood. After assembly it is very difficult to sand with the grain without making cross-grain scratches on the adjoining wood, and these are difficult to remove.

All edging adjacent to the top of thin veneer plywood or plastic laminate must be sanded before the top is attached, or you risk damaging the veneer or plastic.

After assembly and before you start finishing, go over the entire piece very carefully. Make sure all nails and screws are perfectly flush with the surface, or are set or countersunk and filled. Repair imperfections like dents, cracks, or gouges. Any remaining glue on exposed surfaces must be removed carefully by peeling or scraping with a sharp knife or scraper. (Trying to sand off dried glue makes a mess.)

A scraper like the one shown here is even better than a very fine sandpaper, and can be used in many places. By pulling it along with the grain while applying pressure you will smooth the wood without getting dust in the pores.

Most other minor imperfections will succumb to the careful but thorough use of sandpaper. First use a medium grade to re-move blemishes like saw, plane, or hammer marks, and then a fine grade for final smoothing. Always sand with the grain and use a sanding block whenever possible.

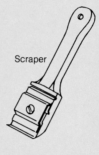
Scraper

Sealing

Basically, a sealer is any substance that can seal or partially seal the wood's pores. Applying a thin coat of sealer before staining or painting usually ensures a smoother and more professional finish, because it hardens the softer grains and lets the wood take stain or paint evenly. This is especially useful for finishing softwoods like fir, and porous woods like maple and oak. Sealer is also applied after staining or filling to protect the stain and filler from subsequent finishing coats.

Read the directions on the label before you buy or use any sealer. They are made for different purposes and are applied differently. Always sand the sealer carefully when it is completely dry.

Filling

Filling is only necessary if you want a deep, glossy, glass-like finish. If you want a natural-wood look, you won't need a filler.

Oak, walnut, mahogany, and other large-pore woods need a thick, heavy filler; small-pore woods like maple or birch need lighter filler. Check with your dealer and read the label on any filler product before you start.

Stains

If you want a transparent finish that shows off the beauty of the natural wood, you may want to use stain. For walnut, mahogany, and other dark woods, a transparent oil or varnish finish is all that is needed. For lighter woods, some sort of stain will bring out their color and add vitality.

Some porous woods, as we mentioned, take stain more even-ly if a thin coat of sealer is applied first. Always use sealer on any end grain so it won't absorb too much stain.

There are five basic kinds of stains: water stains, pigmented oil stains, penetrating oil stains, nongrain-raising stains, and spirit stains. Following is a very general introduction to the ones we think are best for home use. Make sure you read and understand the directions on any stain you buy.

Pigmented oil stains. These are the best for home workshop use. They are available in the widest variety of colors at reasonable cost, and you can modify them yourself by adding small amounts of painter's pigments. Their penetration is shallow so they can be worn or sandpapered through more easily than other stains.

Stir pigment stains thoroughly and often, as the pigments tend to settle out. Apply them with a full brush or cloth, and wipe off the excess with a soft cloth—going with the grain to avoid cross-grain streaks.

Pigment stains can be thinned as necessary with turpentine or paint thinner, and they mix readily with fillers. They are easy to apply, and you can control their intensity somewhat by rubbing with a soft cloth. As restaining is difficult, be sure to test for the proper color before you stain your project.

Water stains. These are dyes mixed in water, which are applied and allowed to dry on the wood. Some come in powder form and others come ready-mixed. They are odorless, contain no flammable liquids, and clean-up is done with soap and water. Furthermore, they tend to penetrate the wood uniformly—even fir, maple, and oak—which makes presealing unnecessary.

However, water stains tend to raise the grain. This can be overcome by sponging the project with plain water, letting it dry, and sanding it smooth again before applying the stain.

Before you stain your project, try the water stain on a test piece and let it dry thoroughly to see if you like the result. Use a full brush to apply the stain and let it dry before proceeding. Several coats of thin stain are preferable to a single coat of strong color.

Penetrating oil stains. These are oil-soluble stains dissolved in a natural or synthetic oil base and are actually one-step finishes, as they stain and penetrate the wood with resin or a synthetic plastic, sealing the wood but still giving the natural texture and feel of open grain. Penetrating oil stains are also called plastic oil sealer stains, penetrating wood sealer stains, tung oil stains, and Danish oil stains.

Apply the oil stain with a clean rag, let it set long enough to penetrate the wood, and then remove the surplus and even out the color with the same cloth. Make your last wipe with the grain.

Final finishing

The final finish is the last thing you apply to your project and the one that gives it luster and protection. Varnish, plastic, shellac, lacquer, wax, and oil are all transparent finishes through which you can see the natural or stained color of the wood. Again, talk with your dealer and read the label before you use any of these products.

Varnish. Until plastics, varnish was the most used, practical, and durable of all the finishes, and many kinds and brands are available. The glossy ones are the toughest and the clearest. The satin finishes contain a little pigment that clouds them.

For the first coat, use a sealer or thin the varnish with turpentine. Rub the dry layer with fine steel wool and then apply at least three finish coats. For a hand-rubbed, satin appearance, make the last coat a satin-finish varnish or rub the last glossy coat with rottenstone or pumice in oil or water.

Plastic. The synthetic or plastic varnishes are made for specific uses, so be sure to read the labels. Most of them are easier to apply, last longer, and make a better surface than the old natural oil-resin varnishes.

Most plastic finishes are still oil-based, although in some areas a water emulsion system of sealer, stain, and plastic finish is available. These finishes meet all the latest government environmental standards, are the easiest to apply, and give a beautiful finish. Furthermore, they contain no turpentine or other volatile solvents, and they clean up with water.

Shellac. This is one of the most beautiful finishes for wood, but its disadvantages often outweigh its beauty. It is alcohol-based, so it dissolves if a cocktail or wine is spilled on it. Ammonia, soap, detergent, and even the hard water in some areas of the country will damage the surface.

Shellac is easy to apply and dries dust free in about 30 minutes. Scratches and blemishes are easy to repair if you know how. Learning about the uses of shellac will be helpful if you will be doing a lot of furniture finishing.

Lacquer. Lacquer has an acetone base and dries even faster than shellac. Spray lacquers dry in about 10 seconds; brushing lacquer contains more acetone and takes a little longer, but not much. It might be fun for you to learn about and experiment with lacquer if you are really interested in furniture finishing or refinishing. For occasional finishing it is not worth the trouble.

Wax. A wax finish gives wood a delightful soft luster, but it

doesn't seal the wood as varnishes do, and it needs to be buffed regularly and replaced every few years to keep its original beauty. It also needs a close-grained or well-filled and sealed wood to work properly. It will not polish well on coarse-grained woods.

Oil. The traditional oil finish is boiled linseed oil, either mixed half-and-half with turpentine, or heated to make it thin enough to use. It is applied with a brush, allowed to soak, and then rubbed until dry with a soft cloth. Several applications are needed over a period of days or weeks, and then an occasional application for the life of the piece. It makes a beautiful finish, but is tedious to use.

Danish oil is durable and is the easiest to use. Its application is discussed under penetrating oil stains, and it is available with or without pigment. It gives a beautiful, natural look.

Mineral oil is a good, nontoxic finish to use on projects for young children or for food preparation. Let it penetrate the wood, then rub off the excess and buff the surface with a soft cloth. Repeat the application from time to time to keep the project looking its best.

Paint. Don't expect paint to cover blemishes or sloppy work just because it's opaque. Sand and prepare a piece for painting as carefully as you would do for staining and varnishing. Nail holes and cracks or gouges must be filled carefully and sanded smooth.

The pronounced hard and soft grain pattern of fir plywood will show through even several coats of paint unless it is sealed properly. Apply a coat of sealer and sand lightly before applying the primer and finish coats of paint.

On all woods and for all paints, one or more coats of primer should be applied before two coats of color. Use the sandpaper on all but the final coat of paint to ensure smoothness.

A

Arbor. The spindle or shaft that supports the blade or bit in a boring or cutting tool.

Awl. A pointed tool for scribing lines or making pilot holes.

B

Bead. A narrow molding often used to hold glass or a panel in a frame.

Frame
Bead
Glass or panel

Bevel. A surface cut at an angle across a piece of wood.

Bit. The working or cutting part of a tool that's usually removable.

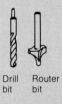

Drill bit   Router bit

Block plane. A hand tool designed to trim end grain, like miter joints, and do other fine work.

Block plane

Brace. A support used to hold a part firmly in place.

Corner brace

Brad-point bit. This makes a clean, circular, flat-bottomed hole that is good for counterboring screws and plugging the holes.

C

Carbide-tipped blade. A saw blade with brazed-on tungsten-carbide tooth tips. These blades last about ten times longer between sharpenings than other blades, and are especially good for cutting hard woods, particle board, and plastic laminates.

Carbide tipped saw teeth

Catch. A device to hold a door closed.

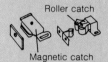

Roller catch

Magnetic catch

Chamfer. A beveled surface cut on the corner of a piece of wood.

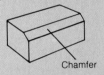

Chamfer

Clamp. A device with movable jaws for holding or pressing parts together.

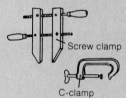

Screw clamp

C-clamp

Cleat. A piece of wood attached to a surface as a support or to strengthen.

Cleat

Shelf cleat (in notches)

Close grain. The term for fine-textured or small-pored woods. Pine and birch are examples.

Coping saw. A hand saw with a thin replaceable blade and a bowed frame, used to cut curves.

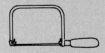

Counterbore. To bore a hole to accept the head of a screw that will be sunk below the surface.

Plug

Counterbore for screw

Countersink. To set a nail or drive or screw below the surface for concealment. To chamfer around the edge of a pilot hole with a cone-shaped bit to bring the head of a screw flush with or below the surface.

Countersunk screw

Cross-cut. To saw a piece of wood perpendicular to the grain.

D

d. The abbreviation of the term "penny," used to designate the size of nails.

Dado. A rectangular groove cut across the grain in a board. Sometimes a groove parallel with the grain is referred to as a dado, but this is not technically correct. (See groove.)

Dado joint. A joint in which one piece of wood is dadoed to accept the edge of another piece.

Dowel. A small-diameter wooden rod, or small sections of such a rod, used to support shelves or reinforce joints.

Dowel cap. Specially cut decorative cap to fill the hole created by a counterbored screw.

Dowel jig. A device used to place holes accurately when making a dowel joint.

Dowel joint. A butt joint using dowels for reinforcement.

Dowel pin. A short length of dowel placed in a hole to support a shelf or other object.

Dowel pins

Drill and counterbore bit. This bit drills a pilot hole, shank clearance hole, and counterbore all in one operation, and must match the screw size. A plug cutter goes with it to fit the counterbore hole.

E

Edging. Strips of wood used to conceal the end grain of boards or plywood, or to protect and conceal the edge of a plywood or plastic-laminate top on a table or desk.

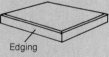

Edging

End grain. The ends of wood fibers that are exposed after a cross-cut.

End grain

F

Face frame. A frame of narrow boards that covers the edge of the top, bottom, sides, and sometimes shelves and partitions of a case or cabinet.

Flush. On the same plane or even with. This usually refers to adjacent surfaces of two or more structural pieces.

Dowel joint. A butt joint using dowels for reinforcement.

Forstner bit. This makes a clean, circular, flat-bottomed hole that is good for counterboring screws and plugging the holes.

G

Grain. The arrangement or direction of the fibers in a piece of wood.

Groove. A channel into which another piece of wood usually fits or works. Technically, this is called a groove when it is cut parallel with the grain, and a dado when it is cut across the grain. However, in practice the words are often used interchangeably.

Groove

H

Hardboard. A panel made from compressed wood fibers, used for cabinet backs and drawer bottoms where a minimum of beauty and structural strength is needed.

Hardwood. The wood of broad-leafed, often deciduous, trees like oak and maple, as opposed to the wood of conifers like pine and fir. Not necessarily a reference to the actual hardness of the wood.

I

Interior grade. Usually refers to plywood that is bonded with glues that are not water resistant.

J

Jig. A device that guides a tool, usually in a cutting or drilling operation, so two or more pieces match or fit together (see dowel jig).

Joint. The junction or connection of two pieces of wood, or the manner in which they are joined.

K

Kerf. The cut made by a saw; technically, the space left between the pieces after the saw blade passes through.

Kerf

L

Lag screw. A screw, usually large, with a square or hexagonal head designed to be driven with a wrench.

M

Miter. A bevel to make a miter joint; any oblique cut on a board.

Miter

Miter joint. The joining of two pieces of wood beveled at the same oblique angle to conceal the end-grain of both pieces.

Molding. A strip of wood used to cover exposed edges or as a decoration.

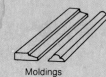

Moldings

Mortise. A cutout in a piece of wood, often used to recess hardware or to accept the tenon in a mortise-and-tenon joint.

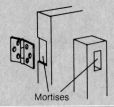

Mortises

N

Nominal size. The rough-sawed size by which lumber is sold, like 1 by 4 (see page 00).

Notch. A cutout in the edge of a piece of wood, usually made across the grain.

Notch

O

Ogee. The s-shaped profile of a particular molding, or the blade to shape an edge or molding in this manner.

On center. The measurement for spacing parts in a project from the center of one to the center of the next.

Open grain. The term for coarse-textured or large-pored woods. Oak and walnut are examples.

P

Particle board. Panels made from compressed wood chips and adhesive.

Penny. The term used to indicate nail lengths.

Piano hinge. A hinge that extends the full length of a door (see page 85).

Pilaster. The perforated metal standard, used with clips, to support adjustable shelves.

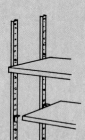

Pilot hole. A hole drilled to guide a screw or nail, which makes driving easier and minimizes splitting.

Plastic laminate. Thin, durable sheets of surfacing material composed of several layers bonded together by heat and pressure. Some examples are Formica, Micarta, Nevamar.

Pumice. A finely ground volcanic rock used to reduce the gloss of a shiny wood finish.

Q

Quarter-round. A molding that is a quarter circle in profile.

R

Rabbet. A step-shaped cut made at the edge of a piece of wood, usually to join the edge of another piece.

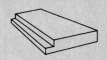

Radial arm saw. A versatile power tool that has a motor and arbor attached to an adjustable arm above a table. In addition to circular saw blades, attachments are

available for a multitude of cutting, shaping, and drilling operations.

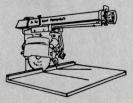

Raised grain. The condition in which the hard grains in wood are raised above the soft grains, usually caused by exposure to moisture.

Resin. Translucent or transparent natural or synthetic materials used to make wood finishes. They are soluable in oil-based liquids, but not in water.

Rip. To saw a piece of wood parallel, or nearly so, to the direction of the grain.

Rottenstone. A finely ground silica containing some limestone; used for polishing wood finishes.

Round over. To remove the corner on a piece of wood by shaping the edge with a router, sander, or rasp.

Rout. To cut grooves, mortises, and notches or to shape edges with a router or with any other tool.

Router. A power tool that cuts grooves, mortises, notches, and shapes edges of wood with a variety of interchangeable bits.

S

Saber saw. A portable power tool with a narrow reciprocating blade, usually used to cut curves. Also called a jig saw.

Setting nails. Countersinking or driving nails below the wood's surface, usually with a nail set or larger nail.

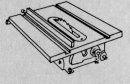

Nail set   Setting a nail

Shape. To cut a contour into the edge of a board or piece of molding. Round-overs and ogees are examples.

Shim. A thin piece of material used to fill out space or add width to a part.

Skirt. The board that hangs directly beneath the perimeter of a table-top or other piece of furniture.

Skirt

Softwood. The wood of conifers like pine and fir, as opposed to the wood from broad-leafed trees like oak and maple. Not necessarily a reference to the actual softness of the wood.

Square. An L-shaped or adjustable device used to lay out or test right-angles and sometimes other angles.

Bevel square

Combination square

Framing square

Stopped. The ending of a chamfer, rabbet, or groove that doesn't run the full length or width of a piece of wood.

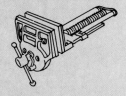

T

Table saw. A power tool that has a motor and arbor beneath a table. Circular saw blades and other attachments protrude above the table for cutting and other operations.

Taper. A gradual and uniform decrease in size from one end to the other, as on a table leg.

Tenon. A projection on the end of a board that fits into a mortise in a mortise-and-tenon joint.

Mortise-and-tenon

Toe nail. To drive a nail through a surface at an oblique angle.

Toe-nailing

Tongue-and-groove. A joint in which a projection or tongue on the edge of a board fits into a corresponding groove on another.

True. To make the surface of a board straight, square, level, or otherwise exact in its relation to another surface.

V

Veneer. A thin surface-layer of wood that adds beauty or durability to less desirable lumber or plywood. Also, any of the thin layers within plywood.

Vise. A bench-mounted clamp to hold a workpiece.

W

Wall anchors. Devices used to attach objects to hollow or masonry walls when nails or screws won't hold.